Designed by Thijs Postma
Translated by Sidney Woods

Most of the photographs and illustrations in
this book come from the author's collection.

© 1979 Fokker bv Schiphol Netherlands.

Originally published in 1979 by Unieboek bv
Bussum as *Fokker bouwer aan de wereldlucht-
vaart*.

This English translation copyright © 1980
Jane's Publishing Company Limited.

First published in the United Kingdom in 1980
by Jane's Publishing Company Limited, 238
City Road, London EC1V 2PU.

ISBN 0 7106 0059 3

Published in the United States of America in
1980 by Jane's Incorporated, 730 Fifth Avenue,
New York N.Y. 10019.

ISBN 0 531 03708 0

Computer Typesetting by Method Limited
Woodford Green, Essex

Printed in Great Britain by
Hazell, Watson & Viney Limited,
Aylesbury, Bucks.

Thijs Postma

Aircraft Builders to the World

JANE'S
LONDON · NEW YORK · SYDNEY

FOREWORD

Sixty eventful years of Dutch aviation history now lie behind us. Sixty years in which our Company has made a considerable contribution to the development of aviation around the world.

Enthusiasm, knowledge, inventiveness, and a natural, inborn urge to do business with the whole world, are the foundation stones on which Fokker's successes are based.

To survive through six decades – and what is more – to have led the field in a branch of industry marked by a continuous and irresistible process of renewal, this is indeed an unbelievable accomplishment.

The days of the 'Spin', F.VII, the D.XXI and the G.1, to mention just a few of the highlights, are only just a life-span behind us. But in particular these aircraft, and the many hundreds of designs which the business genius Anthony Fokker created, form the historical basis of our Company. And, no doubt, the present and future projects will carry on with the Fokker tradition in the decades which lie ahead of us.

An industry which – in spite of all the problems, by virtue of its great successes – has been able to stay on top for sixty years, is really worthy of such a future.

Whatever happens, that future cannot be made safe without great efforts by ourselves.

To this end teamwork, enthusiasm, inventiveness and commercial insight will be essential.

F. Swarttouw,
Chairman

5

INTRODUCTION

The research and the writing of this history of Anthony Fokker and the Fokker Factory has been one of the most pleasant tasks in my life.

Not only because the story of this man and the factory is so fascinating, but more so, because I received so much sympathy and help during my research from Fokker employees (both active and retired). It shows just what kind of spirit prevails in the Fokker factory today, that everybody was prepared to help and that they are all proud of 'his' or 'her' factory.

The greatest problem was: What to put in the book, and what to leave out. Fokker's career began almost at the same time as aviation itself. If I were to describe the complete and unabridged Fokker history right down to the minute details, including all aircraft types, it would become encyclopedic.

This book provides a highly illustrated guide to what has happened since the foundation of the Fokker Factory in 1919. Because Fokker had already made history in Germany before that, I have covered the preceding period as well.

From the unique archives of Holland's first aviation journalist, Mr. Henri Hegener, which came into my possession upon his death, appeared a wealth of documents and information. The very many conversations which I had with Mr. M. Beeling (the man who personally witnessed a great number of the events described in this book), made a number of facts clear to me.

I would like to thank the following persons and institutes (in alphabetical order) for the co-operation which they rendered in the form of photographs, information or research for this book:- P. Alting, Aviodome, Ing M. Beeling, G.C. Dik, Photographic Section Fokker, the many collaborators who have given so much aid:- F. Gerdessen, H. Hooftman, KLM, Photographic Dept., Royal Netherlands Air Force, Department for War History; The Office for Maritime History of the Naval Staff, G. v.d. Meulen, Ing W.S. Nikilujuw, H.J. Nowarra, H.F.V.M. Schwing, Ing H.A. Somberg, W.Th. Vredeling.

Finally I would like to thank my wife Marja, without whose help I would never have completed this book.

In 1976 the first F.28 Mark 4000 was delivered to Linjeflyg of Sweden. The aircraft is identical to the Mark 6000, but has no leading edge slats. At present the Mk. 4000 is the most important aircraft of the F.28 versions in production.

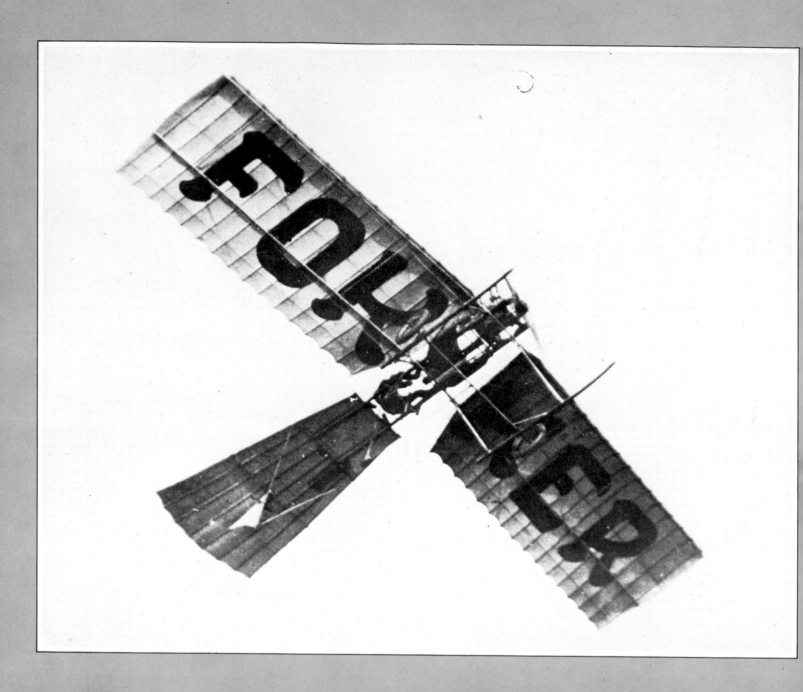

CONTENTS

Left above: Fokker's Spin (Spider) completed in 1910.
Below: Project study for the F.29.

Tïen Seng 成天 PHOTOGRAPHER SINGAPORE.

Fokker's Youth

Anthony Herman Gerard Fokker was born on April 6th, 1890 at Kediri (Blitar), on Java in the Dutch East-Indies and began his life on his father's coffee plantation.

When Tonny was four years old, his parents decided to return to Holland, so that he and his elder sister could receive a proper education. They settled in Haarlem in August 1894.

The ensuing years at school were not particularly enjoyable, neither for his parents nor for Tonny himself. He would only devote his attention to those matters which he considered important – small steam engines, his electric train, and his home-made canoe, but definitely not to his lessons at school. Had he applied the same energy and inventiveness which he now applied to the evasion of education, to his school lessons he could have passed his final exams easily. As it was, he caused his tutors sheer desperation. When he applied to the head-master to have some time off to work on an invention, saying "I'm not learning anything and can do no good here", the headmaster could only agree with him.

Fokker's 'invention' was an explosion-proof tyre, which he and his friend Frits Cremer had developed, but a similar French patent already existed, and nothing came of their application.

1. Fokker – 6 years old – together with his sister in Singapore.
2. Fokker's sister, his mother (who meant a great deal to him) and Tonny himself.
3. Tonny during his school years.
4. Fokker: 18 years old – much against his usual self – for once in a decent suit.
5. Anthony Fokker and Fritz Cremer with their invention: – the explosion-proof tyre.
6. Fokker sailing his boat 'Equilibrist' in the river Spaarne in 1908.
7. A bill made out by Fokker to his own mother for the repair of a water-tap.
The small paper models shown here, were discovered much later in his career in the family attic by his mother.

11

Fokker piloting the 'Sturmvogel' built by Jacob Goedecker, who had helped Fokker to build the second Spin.

The aeroplane built by the pupils of the Dotzheim flying school at Zahlbach. The alleged 'pilot', Bruno Buechner, was unable to take off at the first test; neither could he stop or turn. A resounding smash at the end of the field meant the end of the pupils' dreams.

Predecessor of the Spin. On the back of this unique photograph was written "Baden-Oos 1910". No further details are known of this engineless aeroplane.

Fokker's first "Spin" without a rudder.

Tonny managed to evade his Army conscription by feigning unfitness; but what could he do next? Although he was not in the least worried about his future, his family were, and his father was therefore happy when his son agreed to attend an automobile trade school in Bingen, Germany.

Together with a school-pal (Thomas Reinhold), the 20-year-old Tonny left for Germany. The "automobile trade school" was a farce. In a letter of June 30th, 1910, he wrote to his Mother: "In the afternoon we went to have a look in the driving school. A small square garage with two cars: one contraption with four cylinders and one single-cylinder job, then a lot of scrap iron, impossible to drive and without tyres. Everything in the prospectus had been exaggerated to such extent that I was flabbergasted".

Tonny had already discovered something far better, a driving school at Zahlbach near Mainz, which also had a syllabus for aeroplane construction and a pilots' course, due to start in October. Father Fokker succumbed. The school's pupils were to build their own aircraft under the guidance of a certain Bruno Buechner, who professed to be an "aviator", but who – as it transpired later – had still to learn all about it. After building their first machine, which was too heavy, the pupils built a second and lighter aircraft, only to see it demolished by Buechner at the first test.

Anthony Fokker dried his tears and decided to build his own aeroplane. A fellow-pupil from the school at Zahlbach, the 50-year-old Lieutenant von Daum, became his partner, donating the cash for the engine, and Fokker contributed his knowledge, his labour and 1500 Marks. The machine, named the 'Spin' (Spider), was constructed in an empty Zeppelin shed at Baden-Baden. By the end of 1910 it had been completed, and Fokker was able to make the first hops in it. To start with, the 'Spin' had no rudder, but this did not matter to Tonny, who went almost out of his mind with joy.

At Christmas he went home, only to be greeted with the sad tidings that von Daum had tried to fly the 'Spin' in Fokker's absence and smashed into the only tree on the airfield during take-off. Tonny's parents had the greatest difficulties keeping their son at home.

Letter from Tonny to his mother, asking her to speak to his father on his behalf so that he would be given 150 Marks for an "educational journey" to the Paris Air Show. To "soften the blow" he suggests a visit to his parent's house on the return journey to Germany.

D.M. Your letter and postcard receiv[ed]
Am very busy with the manoeuvr[es.]
Worked 4 whole days at the engine [of]
Goed.'s aeroplane. My aeroplane is not [yet]
finished, and – as it turned out – it w[as]
much better this way.
Wanted to fly to Dietz, but was forced ba[ck]
by strong winds in the Taunus. Other pil[ots]
landed before reaching the Taunus. I fl[ew]
back to Mainz. Tonight, if weather goo[d,]
I'll try again.
Please send large key to second money-b[ox]
as my own is broken (By return P'se). W[ill]
write more soon. If you don't hear from [me]
then everything is o.k. Greetings,
Ton[ny]

Yesterday and day before I made a f[ew]
flights. It has started to rain and stor[m.]
Transporting the 'plane to Mainz by c[ar.]
Letter will follow soonest as I get hom[e.]
21st Sept. Thursday, 19[11]

Last night flew across the Taunus. Cou[ld]
not, after flying 55 minutes, reach Di[etz]
owing to darkness and fog. Landed at Lo[ch-]
rheim, spent the night at Dietz, and start[ed]
from there at 7 in the morning. Due to f[og]
could not find the landing ground a[nd]
landed to ask the way. After that flew [on]
given directions only and landed on the a[ir-]
field. Height 800 metres, 8 to 10 miles wi[nd]
in the Taunus. This evening made seve[ral]
short trips. Tomorrow one short flight a[nd]
then back to Mainz.
Adieu   Fokker   19 Sept. 19[11]

*Postcards sent to his parents' house in Se[p-]
tember 1911. (Translation above)*

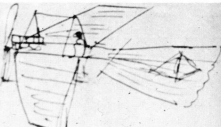

*Small sketch of his third Spin, drawn by Fo[k-]
ker on one of his letters to his home.*

Avia, June 1st, 1911.

Our compatriot Mr A. H. G. Fokker, who is 21 years old, has bee[n]
on the Mainz airfield.
On the 16th of May he made his first flight for the pilot's licence an[d]
with full colours, in spite of the unfavourable weather.
He appeared to be in complete control of his home-made monopl[ane]
having obtained his licence, he took off once more, this time with [an Aus-]
trian officer von Daum as a passenger.
As there are only a few competent pilots in Holland and the partic[ipation]
foreign pilots is always needed at Dutch flying exhibitions, we hope [Fok-]
ker will soon be able to demonstrate his flying skills in this count[ry.]

14

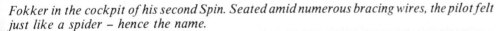

Fokker's Pilot's Licence, dated June 7th, 1911. The tests took place on May 16th, 1911.

The second Spin. Fokker did the tests for his pilot's certificate on this aircraft.

Fokker in the cockpit of his second Spin. Seated amid numerous bracing wires, the pilot felt just like a spider – hence the name.

Thus Fokker was robbed of his second opportunity to fly. However, he immediately set to work on a new aircraft, at Nieder-Walluf on the Rhine, with the help of boat-builder Jacob Goedecker, who also wanted to fly. It was on this second Spin that Fokker taught himself to fly on the Grosser Sand at Gonsenheim. At the beginning of May 1911 he flew a few curves, following them with a complete circle a few days later. On May 12th von Daum finally got his money's worth when Fokker took him along as a passenger.

Another goal was reached on May 16th, when Anthony Fokker obtained his pilot's licence. He had agreed with von Daum that the latter would become the owner of the aircraft as soon as Fokker had gained his licence. Von Daum wanted to start training right away, but Fokker tried to talk him out of it because he had received an invitation from his former home, Haarlem, to give a flying demonstration on the Queen's Birthday. There was money to be made, and he was afraid that von Daum would crash "his" aircraft again.

However, von Daum could not be dissuaded. After a reasonable start to his flying attempts he suddenly seemed to forget everything he had previously learned, and dived into the ground from a height of 10 metres. He shook the bits and pieces from him, and advised Fokker to "take his damned aircraft away, and fly to hell with it". Fokker purchased von Daum's share in the venture for 1200 Marks, and so became the owner of the wreckage and, more importantly, the 50 h.p. Argus engine.

Meanwhile, a third Spin was being made by Goedecker, and on August 31st, 1911 Fokker gave his first flying demonstration over Haarlem. The public went berserk. For Fokker this was the biggest moment of his life: He had left Haarlem as a failure and returned a hero. However, glory did not fill the coffers. A difficult period was looming, but fortunately his first customer for an aircraft and flying tuition arrived. This was none other than Fritz Cremer, his old school pal, with whom he had worked on the explosion-proof tyre. He also made some money giving flying instructions to Goedecker. Towards the end of 1911 Fokker left for Johannisthal, near Berlin, then the Mecca of German aviation.

NIEUWE HAARLEMSE COURANT, September 1st, 1911.

Fokker flew over Haarlem

Today one can hear the same question throughout Haarlem: "Did you see Fokker?" To be honest; I'd never heard of Fokker before. As time goes by you get to know all the celebrities in aviation, but this Haarlemmer was unknown among the big names. However, he is worth mentioning after having seen him fly over the town. My word, what a fuss and noise it caused when that pretty little aeroplane, the "Spin" – which he built himself – flew over the city quietly, serenely and majestically. From every nook and cranny people appeared to watch this miracle, and a miracle it really was. The trams stopped, the kitchen-maids let the steaks burn and the sick people in the hospitals crawled to the windows to watch him. So safe and secure, turning so beautifully and flying so peacefully, the bird-like aeroplane flew over the town and the market; it gracefully circled the steeple of the St Bavo. It astounded one and all. I saw elderly people with tears in their eyes because they had witnessed this miracle. And then there was the pride that it was one of our citizens up there, high in the sky!

I'm told that master Fokker was quite rebellious whilst attending college and that he hated to sit still in class, doing nothing.

Well then, these aviators probably have adventure in their blood.

Fokker also made an altitude flight up to 120 metres. So daring and yet so calm, he stopped his engine at the peak of his flight, descended in a glide, and then switched it on again. The dashing aviator made several turns over the flying field and landed right in front of the flight shed. It was here that the Queen's Birthday Committee waited, not to offer him a laurel wreath, but a bicycle which looked like an aeroplane, abundantly decorated with flowers.

Fokker jumped on the bicycle in high spirits, but could not handle it. "There was too much wind", he said. We can't begin to describe the public's enthusiasm. Fokker lives in all our hearts, not least in that of the little fellow to whom he had given so much pleasure with his flights over the city. Fokker's mother said, emotionally, "I'm glad, my boy, that you are on the ground again".

Anthony Fokker, left, and Fritz Cremer, right, in front of the Spin at the end of the four-day demonstration at Haarlem from August 31st to September 3rd, 1911. (Poster left).

Fokker in his Spin over Haarlem.

THIJS POSTMA

THYS POSTMA

In the Trade Register B of the undersigned Court, on the 22nd of February 1922, the following has been entered: Number 10360. Fokker Aviation Company Limited. Location: Charlottenburg. Purpose of the Company: The application of various inventions, patents and protective rights of Mr Fokker in the sphere of Aerial Transport. The main capital amounts to 20,000 Marks. Managing Director: Doctor at Law Adolf Borchardt, of Charlottenburg. The company is a Limited Company. The Deed of the Company was signed on the 6th February 1912. Apart from the foregoing, the following was announced:- As contribution to the main capital investment, company member Anthony Fokker of Johannisthal has entered his invention: "Automatically Stabilised Aeroplane without mechanical Installation" into the Company, so that the Company has acquired the rights of the patent; even if not applied, the Right of Patent should also be contained in the Applications of Factory Secrets concerning the production of the invention, and is, therefore, laid down as a Factory Secret belonging to the aforementioned Company. The value of this entry has been fixed at 9,000 Marks. This amount is considered to be Company member Anthony Fokker's financial contribution to the main capital. Public announcements concerning the Company will be through the "German Empire Announcer".

Anthony Fokker in his third Spin in front of Goedecker's sheds. Goedecker built the machine in accordance with Fokker's instructions.

Avia, January 15th, 1912

A. H. G. Fokker

Fokker has flown at Johannisthal with great success. Not only is the pilot referred to in highly complimentary terms, but also his machine. The aeroplane is of his own manufacture, and was a great highlight in Haarlem last summer. It appeared to be capable of flying in a very strong wind, and the fact that Fokker was able to fly under such conditions, and perform beautiful flights, pays tribute to the pilot and to his product. Fokker's machine possesses an absolute automatic stability without any mechanical installation.

Avia, February 15th, 1912

Fokker has made an extraordinary flight and an even more extraordinary landing. One afternoon he took off from Johannisthal and set course for Mueggler Lake. At the time a large crowd of skaters was present on the lake, and the crowd was tense because a pilot had announced an intended visit. Suddenly he arrived, carried out some manoeuvres above the icy surface, and landed amongst the skaters. Having remained there for some time – he may even have skated – Fokker departed again "along the same route" as his arrival. It was a sample of perfect airmanship.

Fokker (right) in the third Spin, with Fritz Cremer in the front seat and Th. Reinhold standing.

At Johannisthal, the gods of German aviation flew elegantly, reaped admiration and, what is more, earned money with demonstrations. Fokker, who always looked as if he had been working on his machine nonstop for the last 48 hours, (which was often the case) was observed with pity by the local deities. They had only contempt for his unusual aeroplane, which lacked ailerons, until the moment arrived for his first demonstration. Then everybody was speechless. After one flight he belonged with the greatest.

On February 22nd, 1912, Fokker Aviation Limited was entered in the Trade Register in Berlin, with a capital of 20,000 Marks. In December 1915 the name was changed to Fokker Aircraft Factory Ltd. In the meantime father Fokker had twice put 25,000 Guilders into Tonny's enterprise.

A journey to Russia to sell aircraft to the army was unsuccessful. However, he did get to know the beautiful Ljuba Galanschikoff, who later purchased one of his aircraft and brought much fame to his product, (by improving the altitude record for women in November, for example), and with whom he fell head-over-heels in love. In the meantime Fokker had completed his first military order, for two aircraft. A demonstration tour in the Dutch East Indies by the Dutchman Hilgers brought no business, However, Fokker's flying school was quite successful. Fritz Cremer was chief pilot, and on one day he gave a record number of flying lessons: 38! Another Dutchman, Bernard de Waal, also entered Fokker's Company.

De Luchtvaart, January 20th, 1912

Fokker. With much praise the Berlin press refers to the achievements of our compatriot, Mr Fokker, at Johannisthal, where this dashing aviator passed his flying tests in the same machine in which he flew over Haarlem this summer.

According to the German press the aeroplane, which was constructed by Fokker himself, is able to fly in very strong winds and is more stable in the air than any other type of aeroplane.

To date it is the only aeroplane which has successfully attained absolute automatic stability without any mechanical device, meaning that definite progress has been made in the sphere of flying techniques.

The *Berliner Zeitung am Mittag* reports, among other matters, the following about Fokker:-

"He flew in a rather strong wind in an astonishingly confident manner. In particular the easy control of the machine is exceptional. He flew very narrow figure-of-eights with the greatest ease."

This pronouncement testifies to the success of Mr Fokker.

Fokker Eindecker (Monoplane) over the Western Front.

Fokker too, has crashed

. . . therefore at a quarter past eight o'clock, he took off for the fourth time, on this occasion with Lieutenant von Schlichting as passenger. It was at the stroke of eight o'clock when the accident occurred. Of the various eye-witness accounts which were available, the following is the most acceptable.

The two wings of Fokker's monoplane are each connected to the landing struts by wires; the first wire is connected to the wing-tip, the second to the centre of the wing, whilst the third is connected at a short distance from the frame. While Fokker was circling at a height of approximately 300 metres, the middle wire to the left wing snapped: exactly at the eyelet which connects it to the left wing. It so happened then that the wing – at the place where it had no resistance to offer – began to assume a dome-like shape, so endangering the stability of the aeroplane. Fokker then made his passenger rise from his seat; the passenger then placed his foot on the critical spot in order to render support to the wing. Whether the gusts of wind were too strong, or von Schlichting was unable to maintain his difficult position any longer – which was difficult to determine because the passenger is no longer able to give any evidence whatever is hard to attain. In any case, at a certain moment, 15 metres from the ground, the bearing surface was bent so far that the tip of the wing was pulled inwards. The aeroplane lost its stability and tipped over. Fokker himself was flung out, but was on his feet again very quickly. He only suffered an insignificant wound to his temple. Lieutenant von Schlichting, however, was lying between the remnants of the aeroplane; the engine had smashed his head completely. . .

Excerpt from AVIA-Magazine dated June 1st, 1912. Fokker himself called this the absolute low-point in his life.

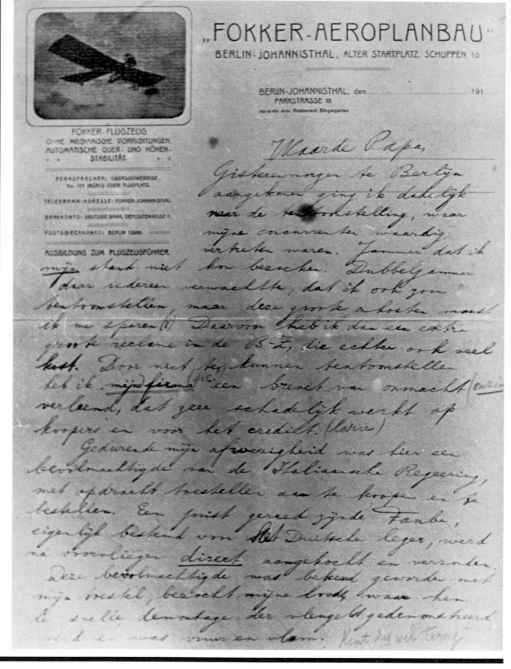

Fokker with his beloved Ljuba Galanschikoff. She was a pilot of international renown, who brought much fame to Fokker through her demonstration flights. Their love died because Fokker could speak of nothing but aircraft.

After his disappointment over the affair with Ljuba, Fokker tried to find consolation in the flashy social life of Johannisthal, but this was not the solution for him.

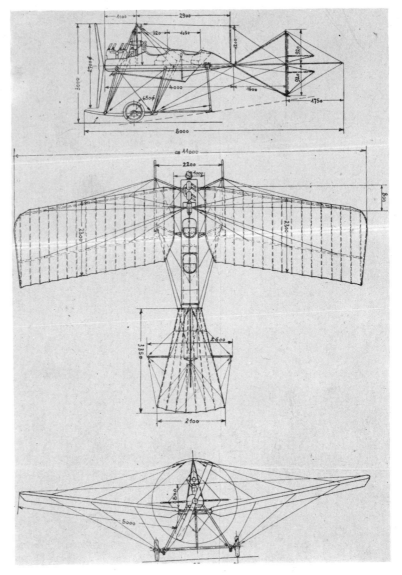

Dear Papa,

After arriving in Berlin yesterday morning I went straightaway to the exhibition, where my competitors were really well represented. A pity that I could not visit *my* stand. The more so, because everybody expected me to exhibit also, but I could meet these large expenses with my savings. For this reason I have inserted extra large advertisements in the B.Z., but these also cost a lot of money. Because I can't exhibit, I have had to give my own firm a Letter of Insolvency which has had a very harmful influence upon any buyers and in getting credit.

During my absence the plenipotentiary for the Italian Government was here, charged with ordering and buying aeroplanes. A Taube, which has just been made ready and which was actually destined for the German Army, was purchased immediately after a presentation flight, and shipped away. This plenipotentiary had gained information about my aeroplanes, and visited my workshops. There, he was shown how fast the wings could be removed and he was really set alight with enthusiasm.

D.T. Letter Card and Picture Postcard received in good order. Good results, but 100 h.p. is also ridiculous. Is the date for Döberitz *still* not settled? Hope the presentation flight is successful and results in orders *which can be fulfilled* in time. Otherwise it's all for nothing.

Naturally, you don't intend to sell that motorcar when it's done it's duties in Döberitz. I would like to know how long it will take for the 50-thousand to have gone. You *excel* at spending, as if it is an art.

In my opinion you will go bankrupt in this manner. If you continue to struggle by yourself then it's a certainty, and I will *not* help you again, even if you stand on your head.

It ought to be pouring with orders for your excellent machines. Now they do nothing but look and copy.

mi adio! All the best.

Right: A variant of the Spin with an enclosed cockpit.
Below: Baroness Leitner's Spin after a cross-wind landing.

Flugplatz Johannisthal.

Fokker-Eindecker in der Kurve

A picture postcard of 1913, depicting a Spin with enclosed cockpit. The military version was called the M.I. This photograph was taken at Johannisthal, but Fokker's military flying school at Schwerin used the same machines.

Bernard de Waal and Küntner in the M.I.

Avia, May 15th, 1913
A nice flight by B. de Waal.

Our countryman, B. de Waal, who is working successfully in Germany, took off from Johannisthal on Tuesday morning at 3.30

The M.II disassembled and mounted on a specially adapted Daimler truck. Fokker's first big order was for ten of these combinations with a total value of 299,800 Marks. The aircraft had a 100 h.p. Argus or Mercedes engine. Its span was 13.2 metres, length 8.5 metres and the maximum speed was 100 km/hr.

Fokker in front of the M.II.

a.m. for a flight to Amsterdam. He was accompanied by a passenger named Küntner. At 6.10 a.m. the aviators made an

A variation of the Spin about which little is known. The fuselage is enclosed, like that of the M.I., but in a totally different manner.

The M.III was much like the M.II, but less streamlined.

The M.IV 'Stahltaube' was not a success.

22

The end of the W.I.

intermediate landing at Hannover, on the Vahrenwalder Heath, departing from there for Utrecht at 9.40 a.m.

A thunderstorm which they encountered between Minden and Osnabrück forced de Waal down, and he was also short of fuel. He therefore landed in the vicinity of Hengelo, from where, at 6.17 p.m., he continued his flight in a westerly direction.

At present, it is not possible to ascertain whether our brave countryman has reached Amsterdam; news is awaited.

Avia, March 1st, 1913

Fokker goes "sea-planing".

Fokker, too, has for some time devoted his attention to the seaplane. Along the Dahme, in the Gronau area, he built a wharf where he constructed two types of seaplane, one of 70 and one of 100 h.p. Fokker has already made several flights with the smaller aircraft, carrying one and two passengers and attaining a speed of 100 km/hr. Work on the aircraft started on the 2nd January, and by the 9th February it was finished. The first flight was then carried out with a passenger and 60 kilogrammes of ballast.

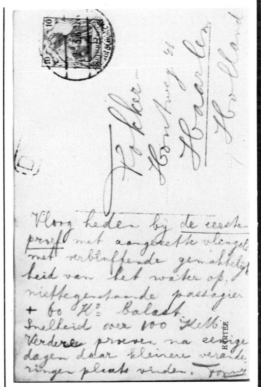

Above: A picture-postcard from Anthony Fokker to his parents, dated February 12th, 1913, reporting his first take-off from water. It reads "Today took off with amazing ease from the water, at first test with the wings installed, in spite of passenger plus 60kg ballast. Speed over 100 km/hr.
Further tests in a few days as a few small changes must be made. Tonny

Take-off of the W.II.

The year 1913 finally brought the orders for which Fokker had hoped for so long. In June the army ordered four aeroplanes of the M.II type, together with their accompanying Daimler lorries and equipment, at a price of 45,700 Marks each. This order was followed one month later by another for six aeroplanes at 19,500 Marks apiece.

The total order, therefore, amounted to 299,800 Marks. Anthony Fokker was rich (at least, he thought so). The idea of having the aeroplane manufacturers located on the same airfield did not appeal to the authorities. If Fokker would move to Schwerin-Görries in Mecklenburg, they said, they could guarantee him 30 pupils a year for his flying school and more orders for aeroplanes. The Schwerin municipality offered him attractive conditions for hiring a piece of ground for use as an airfield, as well as the construction of a factory at 10 per cent of the building costs with the right to purchase.

No matter how attractive this appeared to be, more money was required for extensions and equipment. Father Fokker, together with his brother Edward and Fritz Cremer's father formed a limited company with a capital of 300,000 guilders, to which another 100,000 guilders were added six months later.

The factory now employed 55 persons, and both civil and military orders continued to come in.

The aeroplanes which Fokker built up to 1913 had, more or less, been variants of the Spin. About five examples of the M.I (M = Military) two-seater training aeroplane were built, some of which were for private use. The M.II could be dismantled quickly for transport to the front by lorry. It was for this machine that Fokker received the aforementioned order for ten machines.

The M.III and M.IV which followed were not successful. The M.I to M.IV were designed at the instructions of Fokker by a Mr Palm. With the failure of the M.IV he was fired, to be succeeded by Martin Kreutzer. Fokker's first flying boat, the W.I, crashed during initial tests, and its successor, the W.II, floatplane, made only a few flights before it was dismantled.

Staff of the Fokker Flying School in 1914. From left: Fritz Cremer, Weidner, Fokker (in the cockpit), Bernard (Daddy) de Waal and Küntner.

Above: Fokker performs a loop in an M.VL. A Spin and an M.II are visible in front of the hangar. As can be seen from this photograph, taken in May 1914, Fokker looped at very low altitude.

Below: A collection of Spin, M.I and M.IV aeroplanes at the Fokker flying school at Döberitz. The first armed series of M.Vs went to this school to prepare pilots for service over the front lines.

Avia, May 8th, 1914

Our countryman, A. H. G. Fokker, the famous aeroplane builder living in Germany, again has people talking about him. He is the first in Germany to "tumble" in a completely locally-made aeroplane with a German engine. The aeroplane is powered by a Gnôme engine of 80 h.p. and has great stability, in spite of its low weight of 300 kg. Although Fokker, just like some before him, makes "loops" and figure eights in the air, he should not be described as an aerobat, of which there are so many these days. His tumbling manoeuvres are of a purely scientific nature, and have no other purpose than to investigate the stability of the aeroplane. The same applies to his remarkable flights earlier on at Johannisthal, which were then considered rash and daring. It appears that Fokker plans to show his new aeroplane to the military and scientific authorities.

KAISERLICHES PATENTAMT.

PATENTSCHRIFT

№ 310396

KLASSE 77h. GRUPPE 5.

LUFT-VERKEHRS-G. M. B. H. IN BERLIN-JOHANNISTHAL.

Vorrichtung zum Abziehen von auf Flugzeugen angeordneten Maschinengewehren.

Patentiert im Deutschen Reiche vom 6. Juli 1917 ab.

Die Erfindung betrifft eine Vorrichtung zum Abziehen von auf Flugzeugen angeordneten Maschinengewehren, bei denen der Abzug von einem sich drehenden Teil des Motors aus bewirkt wird, damit zwischen den sich schnell drehenden Flügeln des Propellers hindurchgeschossen werden kann, ohne daß die Geschosse die Flügel treffen. Die dem gleichen Zweck dienenden bekannten Vorrichtungen haben den Nachteil, daß der Abzug nicht immer genau in dem richtigen Zeitpunkt erfolgt und daß ihr Einbau bei den verschiedenen Bau~ ~ von Flugzeugen Schwie~ ~eiten ~ ~oue der Vorrichtung ~um Abzug des ~ ~ewegung

der in die Anfangslage zurückgebracht sind, während Fig. 3 die Vorrichtung mit geöffneter Hebelzange, also in ausgerücktem Zustande darstellt. Fig. 4 und 5 stellen eine abgeänderte Ausführungsform dar.

In Fig. 1 ist *a* die vom Motor angetriebene Nockenwelle, auf der, umgeben von einem Gehäuse *b*, eine Nockenscheibe mit zwei sich gegenüberstehenden Nocken sitzt. Um die Nockenscheibe herum greifen die beiden zangenartig geformten Hebel *c* und *d*, die den gemeinsamen Drehpunkt *f* haben. Etw~ terhalb des oberen Endes des Hebel~ ein Bowdendraht *g* an, dessen H~ seits an einem Stutzen des ~ andererseits an einer ~ gewehres *m* befest~ ~do dos Hol~

The patent recording Fokker's invention of 1915: the synchronised machine gun. This patent was challenged by Swiss-born Franz Schneider, who had patented a similar invention in July 1913. Schneider's invention was based on the blocking of the machine gun when a propeller blade was in front of the barrel. At 1,200 revolutions the machine gun was blocked 2,400 times per minute. The gun, therefore, with its capacity of 600 rounds per minute, was unable to get off a single round. Fokker's device was worked by a camshaft and lever, which fired the machine gun the moment that there was no blade in front of the barrel.

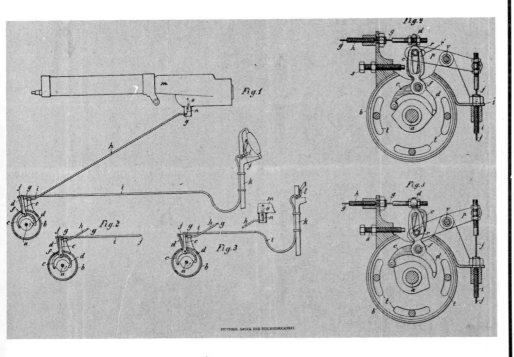

In May 1914 Fokker produced a light, manoeuvrable aeroplane, the M.5. It was designed by Kreutzer and based on a French Morane-Saulnier type H which Fokker had bought second-hand. The machine was built because, in autumn 1913, Fokker had seen the Frenchman Pégoud perform what were, at that time, incredible flying manoeuvres which could not be made by the Spin, (loops etc.). However, Fokker would not have been true to himself if he had not tried to improve on Pégoud. He wrote in his book *The Flying Dutchman,* that he was scared stiff, but he learned – and how! His demonstrations brought him worldwide fame.

The Great War (World War One) changed Fokker's position instantly. On the day war was declared he received a telegram stating that all his available aeroplanes had been requisitioned by the army. The following day a very angry naval officer ordered that all machines should be handed over to the navy.

Fokker wrote: "Every day a crowd of senior army and navy officers came to me, and argued with each other until I thought that Schwerin itself would become a battlefield. They were so heated that they took everything remotely related to an engine or and aircraft. Engines that would have been dumped on the scrapheap a month earlier were now accepted with an alacrity that made them seem like Rolls-Royces."

Elsewhere he wrote: "During my travels I have heard much criticism because I tied my fate to that of the Germans. The allies blamed me for not having placed myself at the disposal of the Entente. These critics did not consider that my own country preferred French aeroplanes to mine, that England and Italy hardly bothered to respond, and that due to the wide-spread corruption I was unable to get started in Russia. Only Germany prepared a good reception for me, even if it was not entirely with open arms."

The first large order came from Austria, and was for a dozen M.7 scouts. Thirty officers entered the flying school, where they were taught to fly by Bernard de Waal and other instructors.

Above: Fokker demonstrates the operation of the synchronised machine gun to the military. A wooden disc was mounted on the propeller to show that the shots were firing between the propeller blades. The aeroplane is a D.1.

Below: The cockpit and synchronised machine gun on a M.5K/MG. The "K" means Kurz = *(short wing) and "MG" means* Maschinengewehr *(machine gun). The supply of cartridges can be seen on the right-hand engine cowling.*

Above: A Morane Saulnier Type N with bullet deflectors on the propeller blades. Flying a similarly equipped Type L two-seater, the French pilot Roland Garros claimed a number of mysterious air victories. As soon as he was within range of the unsuspecting German scouts bullets sped from between his rotating propeller blades. The secret of the steel deflectors was not discovered until April 18th, 1914, when he had to make an emergency landing behind the German lines, and the device fell into German hands before he could burn his machine completely.

Below: A human load on an M.5L. "L" means Lang = *(long wing). Of those standing on the wing, the fifth from the left is Bernard de Waal, identified by his eccentric headgear. Standing, second from right is Küntner.*

Top: The parasol-winged, two-seat M.6 making its debut in June 1914. The machine had an 80 h.p. Oberursel engine. The only one built crashed at Schwerin and was destroyed. Schmidt, Fokker's engineer, is in the cockpit.

Below: An M.7 scout of the Kiel naval air-defence unit. It was for this type of aeroplane that Fokker received his first wartime order. About 20 were built, the first being completed in January 1915.

Top: Germany's first Ace, Max Immelmann. The flight manoeuvre comprising a half roll at the top of half a loop was named after him.

Immelmann flying his E.I. (the later designation of the M.5K/MG) as "top cover" for a Roland C.II-scout. E.I means Eindecker (monoplane) number one. First World War operational aerial photographs are very rare.

Immelmann and Oswald Boelcke were the top-scoring aces at the beginning of the war. Boelcke wrote of an unarmed M.5 in December, 1914: "The Fokker is the nicest Christmas present, in which I take a childish delight." The M.5K/MG, or E.I. had an 80 h.p. Oberursel engine and was armed with an LMG 08 machine gun. Span 8.95m, length 6.75m, height 2.88m. Maximum speed was 130 km/hr.

This experimental fighter, the M.9, also called K.1 (K = Kampfflugzeug = fighting aeroplane), first appeared in April 1915. In addition to the pilot, two 80 h.p. Oberursel engines were positioned in the central nacelle, and the two fuselages each had an air gunner in the nose. During tests the aeroplane proved useless.

This M.10E two-seat trainer went into service with the Austrians in April 1915, designated B.1.

An M.8(A.1) trainer aircraft and artillery spotter of September 1914. Fokker built 30 to 40 of them, and Halberstadt later built them under license as the Halberstadt A.2. The aeroplane depicted made an emergency landing in the Netherlands and was interned, the orange circle on the wing being the Dutch military insignia.

Wing load-testing of an M.10E. The aeroplane was inverted and the fuselage placed on a couple of trestles. Sand was then poured on to the concave uncovered lower wing surface until the wings failed. In this way the maximum load in kilogrammes could be determined.

The M.16E, of 1915, an experimental fighter with one machine gun, did not go into production.

Fokker with the M.17E, a version of the M.16E with a 100 h.p. Oberursel rotary engine instead of the liquid-cooled Mercedes of the latter. Equipped with one machine gun, the M.17E was not put into production.

Above: The W.3 floatplane, which appeared in March 1915, was a modified M.7 with floats originating from the W.2. After some unsatisfactory trials it was restored to M.7 configuration.

Below: Fokker, who loved water sports all his life, built a frame on the floats of his W.3 and mounted a rotary engine in the stern. This concoction was designated W.4.

The only machine guns available to the Germans were water-cooled, and therefore too heavy to be carried aboard an aeroplane. On the other hand, the British aircraft had light, air-cooled machine guns and gained quite a lot of victories in the first year of the war. Then something happened to change aerial warfare drastically.

A French pilot claimed quite a few victories among his German opponents in an inexplicable manner. As soon as his machine was within shooting distance, a stream of bullets shot through its propeller arc. This baffled the Germans, until the aeroplane landed behind the German lines after being hit by ground fire. Before the pilot, who was none other than the famous Garros, had succeeded in burning his aeroplane, the Germans managed to seize it.

Garros had mounted a machine gun forward of the cockpit (see photograph on page 26, top left) and fitted steel deflectors to his propeller to deflect those bullets which did not pass between the propeller blades. Attempts to copy this simple system failed, because the chromium-steel German bullets, which were harder than the French brass bullets, went right through their own propellers.

Fokker was requested to adapt the system for German use. After two days and nights of work with his collaborators Luebbe, Heber and Leimberger, he demonstrated a synchronising system to the authorities which functioned very well, and which has been used in propeller–driven aircraft ever since. Like all brilliant inventions, this one was very simple. The firing mechanism of the machine gun was linked to the engine by means of a cam-shaft and lever, so that the weapon fired only when there was no propeller blade in front of its barrel. A new department was opened at Schwerin to manufacture the apparatus.

On August 1st, 1915 Lieutenant Max Immelmann achieved his first air combat victory flying a Fokker M.5K/MG, and was followed 18 days later by Boelcke. At the end of October Immelmann and Boelcke gained their fifth and sixth victories respectively. The Fokker monoplanes were causing alarm amongst allied pilots who spoke of the "Fokker scourge." Politician-cum-aeroplane designer Pemberton Billing, in a speech in the House of Commons, stated that British pilots referred to RFC aeroplanes as "Fokker fodder".

M.16Z under construction. Thirty of these two-seaters were used by the Austro-Hungarian army with the designation B.3. The M.16Z had a 160 h.p. Mercedes or a 200 h.p. Austro-Daimler engine. Its predecessor, the smaller M.16E fighter, did not go into production.

The D.II (M.17ZF) fighter, designed by Martin Kreutzer, appeared early 1916 and was completed before the D.I. With a 100 h.p. Oberursel engine it attained a speed of 150 km/hr, and the armament comprised one machine gun. A total of 177 of this type was produced.

The D.I had a 120 h.p. Mercedes engine, but looked very much like the D.II. Martin Kreutzer lost his life whilst testing a D.I. Although 130 were built, the type proved too slow for use on the Western Front.

One of the ten Dutch D.IIIs (M.19Ks) purchased by the LVA (Dutch Aviation Department) in Germany. The orange circles on the aircraft were the Dutch national insignia during World War One. Some 230 were built, but were not successful in spite of the fact that Boelcke shot down six opponents with this type. With a 160 h.p. Oberursel engine the maximum speed was 160 km/hr, and its armament consisted of two machine guns.

The DV (M.22E), armed with a single machine gun, was a design by Reinhold Platz, based on earlier aircraft, who had a hand in earlier aeroplanes.
It was the most manoeuvrable aeroplane of its time, but owing to problems with the Oberursel engine it was not a success. Of the 300 built, most were used for training purposes.

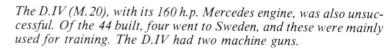

The D.IV (M.20), with its 160 h.p. Mercedes engine, was also unsuccessful. Of the 44 built, four went to Sweden, and these were mainly used for training. The D.IV had two machine guns.

Fokker at his desk.

MURDER, MANSLAUGHTER, OR ACCIDENT.

I do not intend to deal with the colossal blunders of the Royal Flying Corps, but I may refer briefly to the hundreds—nay, thousands—of machines which they have ordered and which have been referred to by our pilots at the front as "Fokker fodder." Every one of our pilots knows when he steps into them that if he gets back it will be more by luck and by his skill than by any mechanical assistance he will get from the people who provide him with the machines. I do not want to touch a dramatic note this afternoon, but if I did I would suggest that quite a number of our gallant officers in the Royal Flying Corps have been rather murdered than killed.

A cutting from The Aeroplane *of 1916. Its title: "Aircraft in the Commons." Speaker: Noel Pemberton Billing.*

Direktor Fokker (×), der Erbauer der neuen deutschen Flugzeuge, neben ihm der Großherzog von Mecklenburg.

Die neuen deutschen Flugmaschinen, die sich den französischen außerordentlich überlegen zeigten, werden in den Fokkerwerken in Schwerin hergestellt. | Der Großherzog von Mecklenburg-Schwerin hat jüngst dem Inhaber der Fokkerwerke persönlich das mecklenburgische Verdienstkreuz überreicht.

The success of Fokker's monoplanes resulted in the order that each allied reconnaissance machine was to be escorted by at least three other fighters, and that, should one of the escorts have to abandon its duty, the reconnaissance was to be aborted.

The Fokker synchronisation system was also installed in other aircraft, and other factories soon started to design and incorporate synchronising systems.

However, the Inspectorate of Flying Troops would not accept responsibility for several synchronising systems, and wanted to keep the device free of the fierce competition between the various aircraft factories.

After various difficulties the production of synchronisation systems was established in a special factory, Aircraft Weapons Ltd (Flugzeugwaffen GmbH) in Berlin-Reinickendorf. They selected the Fokker system (meanwhile improved), and were thus assured of regular production in sufficient quantity.

It was not until 8th April, 1916, that the first Fokker equipped with the synchronisation system fell into the hands of the Allies, but for some time before that a Bristol Scout had already been on trial with a synchronisation system. Meanwhile, new allied aeroplanes arrived at the Front with synchronised machine guns, and Germany lost its advantage in the air. During the Battle of the Somme Allied aircraft could often fly across the German lines unhindered. At the Fokker works it was realised that the Eindecker had had its day, and a number of biplanes were designed. This led to orders for the types D.I. to DV, but these types, generally speaking, had an inferior performance to other fighters with the same engines and were therefore used mainly for fighter pilot training; only small numbers were ordered. To make use of the available production capability at Fokkers, 400 AEG C.4 and C.4A training and reconnaissance aeroplanes were ordered. These machines, just like the Fokker aeroplanes, had tubular steel fuselage frames.

Cutting from the Wiener Extrablatt *of March 3rd, 1916. It reads "Director Fokker (x) the constructor of the new German aeroplanes, in company with the Grand Duke of Mecklenburg.*
The new German aeroplanes, which have so thoroughly proven themselves against the French, are constructed in the Fokker factories in Schwerin. Recently, the Grand Duke of Mecklenburg-Schwerin personally handed the proprietor of the Fokker factories the Mecklenburg Order of Merit."

Top left: Martin Kreutzer in front of a D.I. He lost his life during a test flight in an aeroplane of this type on 27th June, 1916. From the M.5 onwards he had designed all the Fokker aircraft; Fokker merely outlined the intended aircraft. Above: Kreutzer's obituary notice.

Left: Reinhold Platz (right) and Fokker with a Dr.I. Platz succeeded Kreutzer after the latter's death.

The V.1, below, was the first aeroplane completely designed by Platz.

Bottom of page: The V.2 (left) was a development of the V.1, and the V.3 (D.VI) (right) was the first triplane.

Fokker's designer, Martin Kreutzer, died in June 1916 during a test flight in a D.I. Various new designers succeeded him, but none were good enough. Reinhold Platz, a welder who had worked on the steel-tube fuselage of Fokker's Spin as far back as 1912, and who had risen to a position of some importance in the factory, suggested to Fokker that he should take Kreutzer's place. Fokker replied "That's what I thought", and so Platz became the designer of many historic Fokker aeroplanes. He also became the manager of some 1,600 workers.

Like Fokker, he lacked a scientific education and did nothing about learning any theory in later years. Platz's first design, the V.1 (Verspanungslos 1 = cantilever wing), was a very advanced machine for its time, but unsuitable for military purposes. It was purely an experimental aeroplane, as was the V.2, a similar design with an in-line engine. However, an operational success was achieved with the famous Dr.I (Dreidecker I = Triplane 1). The Dr.I had an Oberursel rotary engine of only 110 h.p., but in spite of this its rate of climb was phenominal and the machine was unbelievably manoeuvrable.

At the Inspectorate of Flying Troops there was thought to be potential in a collaboration between Fokker and Professor Hugo Junkers, and in the autumn of 1917 they were persuaded to join forces. However, the two men were too different by nature, age and education, and the "Junkers-Fokker Company" was short-lived.

Top: Fokker in front of the V.1 with (left to right) Miss Guska, Frau Grabitz (Fokker's landlady in Schwerin) and Miss Schöngart, secretary to the Aircraft Armament Factory.

Firing levers for the Dr.I's machine guns. Operation was by thumb-pressure, which meant that the pilot could keep his hands on the control column.

Fokker Dr.I triplanes at the Front. In the background are some tent-hangars.

The Fokker-Dr.I

In the spring of 1917 a new British fighter, the Sopwith Triplane, appeared on the Western Front. It excelled in manoeuvrability and climbing power, and so impressed the German air force that they encouraged their own manufacturers to design similar aircraft. The first prototypes were on order by July 1917.

In June 1917 Fokker's also decided to design a triplane. A demonstration machine, the D.VI biplane (werknummer 1661), was under construction for Austria-Hungary, and this was completed with a third wing. At first this D.VI (which was later designated V.3) had no interplane struts. Its powerplant was the 110 h.p. Oberursel rotary engine (Fokker had a share in the Oberursel Engine Works).

The D.VI was flown by Lt Werner Voss, who was enthusiastic about the type. The Air Force took an interest, and on 14th July 1917 the first batch of 20 triplanes was ordered, including three prototypes, comprising a second D.VI and two V.IVs (later the V.4). The production type was Dr.I (originally F.1). The first D.VI (V.3) triplane was sent to Austria-Hungary after its tests.

The German Air Force had great success with the Dr.I at the beginning of 1918, but the type was out-moded rather quickly because it was too slow. Nonetheless, 320 were delivered.

From April 1918 onwards the Dr.I began to be replaced in front-line units. The most important unit to fly the Dr.I was Jagdgeschwader I (Fighter Squadron I), the so-called "Richthofen Circus."

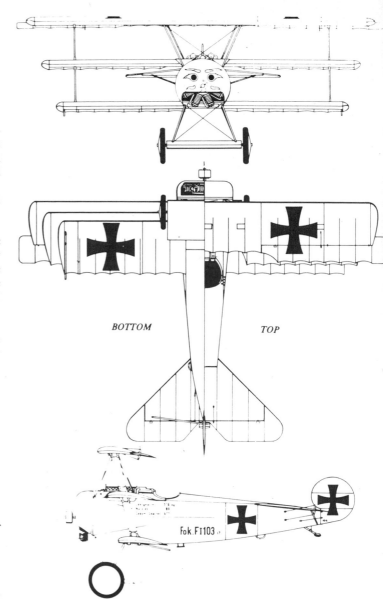

Below: Lt Werner Voss with Fokker. The three-view drawing (top right) depicts his aeroplane. When he was shot down on September 23rd 1917, in aerial combat against an overwhelming number of allied "aces", he had 48 victories to his credit.

Below right: Rittmeister Freiherr Manfred von Richthofen, the highest-scoring fighter pilot of World War One, with 80 victories. Because his machines were bright red he was nick-named "The Red Baron". On April 21st, 1918 he was shot down whilst on the tail of a Sopwith Camel. He was attacked by Roy Brown, a Canadian airman, and at the same time he was shot at from the ground by a machine gun manned by Australians.

The all-red Dr.I of von Richthofen in a dogfight with a Sopwith Pup.

THIJS POSTMA

Fokker=Werke

G.m.b.H.
Schwerin i.M.

Das ideale
Sport=Flugzeug.

The D.VII (also known as the V.6) was a triplane with a 160 h.p. Mercedes engine. Owing to the heavier engine it was a larger aeroplane. It was not satisfactory, and therefore did not go into production.

In September 1917 Fokker produced this monstrosity, the V.8 quintuplane. Presumably he figured that, as his triplane had met with success, more wings would reap more success. After a few short hops it was demolished.

The V.7 an experimental version of the Dr.I, is seen here with a 160 h.p. Siemens-Halske engine and a four-bladed propeller. Four of these machines were built. The first triplane was the D.VI (V.3). The prototypes for the Dr.1 were a second D.VI (V.4) and two V.IVs (V.4s). The D.VII (V.6) was a contemporary design with the 160 h.p. Mercedes. The V.10, also with a 160 h.p. Mercedes, was not completed.

This V.11 was the first prototype for the famous D.VII fighter.

Towards the end of 1917 the V.9 appeared, its fuselage, tailplane and undercarriage being very similar to those of the triplane. The V.9 was entered in a fighter competition, and was the forerunner of the D.VI fighter.

The V.13 was the final prototype of the D.VI fighter. Note the similarity to the V.9. Although the D.VI was used at the Front, it was much inferior to the D.VII.

Left: A Fokker advertisement for "the ideal sports-aircraft" from the Motor magazine of September/October 1919. This "sports" aeroplane is a D.VIII Fighter, complete with military markings.

"In the first place, all D.VII aeroplanes..."

Left: D.VII in flight

With this statement, the Allies ordered the Germans to hand over all Fokker D.VII fighters. It was the only type to be specifically mentioned in the Armistice Agreement.

Below: Three-view of a Dutch D.VII, purchased from Fokker by the Dutch Aviation Department after World War One.

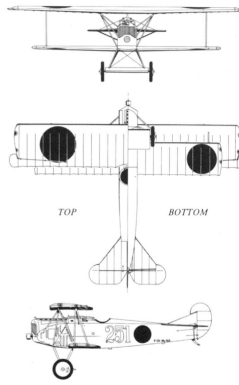

TOP   BOTTOM

The D.VII was the most successful fighter of World War One. Fokker won an order for 400 machines during the fighter competition of January 1918. The V.11, prototype of the D.VII only just met the deadline, and Fokker had had no opportunity to test it, so he was obliged to do this whilst demonstrating it during the meeting.

Its longitudinal stability apparently left much to be desired, and the aircraft would spin at the slightest provocation. Fokker flew the fighter as sharp as a razor, and no-one noticed its short-comings, but he was afraid that the front-line pilots who were going to fly it in the contest would break their necks in it, and so spoil his chances.

On the Saturday he phoned Schwerin and ordered two of his best welders to come over, and the three men worked secretly throughout the night. By Sunday afternoon 60cm had been inserted in the fuselage, and the rudder had been enlarged.

Fokker quickly made a test flight, just before the manufacturers were forbidden to enter the field. The aeroplane was no longer dangerous, but the tail controls were still very sensitive. Fokker handed the machine over to the competition committee and left the field. In his book *The Flying Dutchman* he wrote: "Before I left the field, however, I sauntered over to a group of pilots waiting to test the various aeroplanes. Having talked to them, I took First Lieutenant Bruno Loerzer, the Squadron Commander, aside. "You will observe something special about my aeroplane, Lieutenant", I said, "her fast reaction to control movements makes her extremely manoeuvrable. Please tell this to the others, they can use this information to their own advantage." With this I had warned them to be alert without them realising it, and I left, to all appearances, to seek the sleep which I needed so very much. After this slight hint they demonstrated the aeroplane as well as I could have done – perhaps even better."

D.VIIs under construction at Schwerin.

Below left: Ostdeutsche Albatros-Werke-built D.VIIs behind the Front after the capitulation.

38

Above: An office of the Fokker Factory at Schwerin. This photograph was taken on August 9th, 1918.

Above: The exterior of the factory, again in 1918. Because of continuous extensions it had grown into a conglomeration of buildings. It was said that Fokker built beautiful aircraft in despicable factories.

Below: Captured D.VIIs after the Armistice. The symbol adjacent to the German Balkan Cross is not that of the Polish Air Force, but a German unit emblem.

There was cut-throat competition among the German aircraft factories. Realising the advantages of this, the German authorities decided, towards the end of 1917, to hold a competition for a new fighter. By this means they also hoped to reduce the number of different aircraft types in service. The testing of the competing prototypes had to be as fair as possible, conducted by experienced pilots, and under the continuous control of the technicians of the aircraft repair shops. Three competitions (*D-Flugzeug Wettbewerb*) were therefore held in 1918.

The first, in January and February 1918, resulted in an order for 400 D.VIIs (prototype V.11) from Fokker. The Albatros factories and the East-German Albatros factories gained large orders for the licensed construction of the D.VII, and AEG also received an order but did not supply any aircraft. The D.VI was ordered as stand-by, but due to the success of the D.VII its production was limited. In June 1918, during the second competition, for aeroplanes with a rotary engine, Fokker came second with the V.26, and the type was ordered as the E.V.

Powered by the 110 h.p. Le Rhône engine, the E.V arrived at the Front in July 1918, but fatal accidents quickly occurred due to wing-failure. The investigation of these accidents and the necessary constructional changes meant that the aeroplane, redesignated, VIII, did not return to service until October 1918.

The third competition, in October 1918, was terminated by the end of the war, but the Fokker V.29 and V.36 were well in the running.

During the revolution that followed the ending of the First World War, Fokker managed to escape from his landlady's besieged house by dressing in her son's uniform. Bernard de Waal, who was waiting on a motorcycle, took him to the railway station, from where he escaped to Holland on a goods train.

Some civil aeroplanes were built at Schwerin under the supervision of Platz, but production soon ended, and the Fokker Aeroplane Works, where some 3,350 aeroplanes had been built during the War, was liquidated. It became Schwerin Industrial Works Ltd, producing yachts, motorboats, canoes and, later, bedsteads and scales.

The V.17 with 110 h.p. Oberursel or Le Rhône engine. This modern-looking fighter was Platz's first monoplane, but owing to the low-powered engine its performance was mediocre.

The V.20 was a larger version of the V.17, with a 160 h.p. Mercedes engine. Platz built the aeroplane in 5½ days just before the competition in January 1918, but its performance was disappointing.

The V.21 was a development of the V.20, and participated in the second fighter contest at Adlershof. It was rejected before testing. Like the V.21, the V.23, another monoplane, also had the 160 h.p. Mercedes engine.

The V.25 was a low-wing monoplane. As Director of the Junkers-Fokker factories, Fokker had flown the Junkers D.1. fighter, and ordered Platz to build a similar aeroplane. The 110 h.p. Oberursel engine, however, was not powerful enough.

The prototype of the D.VIII fighter (also called the E.V) was this V.26.

The V.29 was another (larger) version of the V.26. It was not put into production. The engine was a 160 h.p. Mercedes.

The V.27, which appeared in April 1918, was a larger version of the V.26 with a 195 h.p. Mercedes engine.

The V.33 was a development of the V.9. The only example of the type, powered by a 110 h.p. Le Rhône, was used by Fokker until 1922.

40

This aeroplane was designed by Fokker as a flying bomb, to be towed by a D.VII. The military authorities showed no interest, and Fokker exhibited it as a glider at the 1921 Paris Air Show.

Left: After the war, when money devalued daily, some companies including Fokker, were authorised to print their own money for their employees. An equivalent amount in current money was to be deposited in the bank.

Below: The pilots of the 6th Fighter Flight of the Richthofen-Geschwader, are seen seated on the wing of a Fokker D.VIII. In the right foreground is Fokker, and above him, seated, is Lt Neckel, a pilot with 30 victories. Jasta 6 was one of the few units to operate the D.VIII, which was introduced to the Front as the E.V in August 1918. After a number of in-flight wing failures the type was taken out of service, returning to the Front after improvements to the wing had been made. However, it was by then too late for the aircraft to play an important role in the conflict.

The V.34 single-seat fighter appeared in the summer of 1918. Derived from the D.VII, it had a 185 h.p. BMW engine and was not mass-produced.

This armoured "slit-trench" fighter, the V.37, was designed towards the end of 1918.

The V.38 was an enlarged D.VII. It served as the prototype for the C.I scout, which arrived too late at the Front to participate in the War. Fokker took approximately 70 of these with him to Holland.

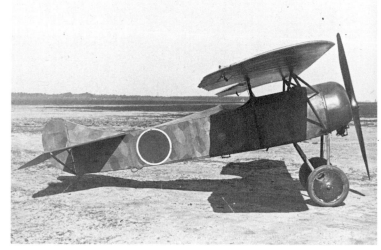

A smaller version of the D.VIII fighter was this V.39 post-war sports aircraft. The V.39 in the photograph has a 110 h.p. Le Rhône engine, but lighter engines were also installed.

The V.40 was an even lighter sports aeroplane than the V.39. Powered by a 35 h.p. Anzani engine, it was the smallest aeroplane ever built by Fokker, but there was no market for the type.

The V.42 glider, one of the last V-types, was sent to Amsterdam and tested as a seaplane.

FOKKER
WERKE G.M.B.H. SCHWERIN MECKL.
ABTEILUNG SCHIFFBAU

Schleppdampfer + Motorboote
Segeljachten

Advertisement from the Motor *Magazine, Jan./Feb. 1919.*

The Dutch Fokker Factory

This is where the history of Anthony Fokker in Germany ends, and the story of the Dutch Fokker Factory begins.

Fokker himself said:-

"Almost before I realised what happened, I was climbing the ladder faster than my feet could carry me".

Fortunately Fokker was not only a remarkable fighter designer. As will be seen later, his commercial aircraft would also become renowned all over the world, but now they would come from Holland.

Fokker's return to Holland was quite spectacular. When the war had ended, the Netherlands Automobile and Aircraft Industries Trompenburg Ltd had received an order from the Dutch Government for the manufacture of 200 aircraft; 118 scouts and 98 fighters. After the Armistice the orders were cancelled, but the Dutch Government was obliged to purchase all materials to a value of 5.5 million Dutch florins. Fokker heard about this contract, and managed to take over part of it. Fokker supplied 20 D.VIIs and 59 C.1s (including spares for another 20 aircraft) to the Dutch Military. Another 20 D.VIIs and 5 C.1s went to the Dutch Navy Air Department and 6 D.VIIIs to the Royal Dutch East-Indies Army. Immediately upon the cessation of hostilities Fokker hid the majority of the materials from his German factories (i.e. 220 aircraft and 400 engines) in farms, cellars, remote sheds and barns, making sure that sufficient aircraft, engines and machines remained to be destroyed by the special Allied demolition groups. Under the leadership of Heinrich Mahn, head of the Transportation Department of the Fokker Factory, a colossal smuggling operation was organised. Within six weeks, using 350 railway freight-cars, no fewer than 200 aircraft, 400 engines, 100 parachutes and an enormous quantity of materials and tools were smuggled across the border into Holland. Everything was temporarily stored at the Amsterdam petrol harbour.

Albert Plesman, a young lieutenant in the Dutch Aviation Department, together with his colleague Hofstee and with the support of the Supreme Commander of the Dutch Military Forces, General Snijders, organised the first Air Traffic Exhibition in Amsterdam (ELTA). Within five months an airfield and exhibition halls were constructed in the North of Amsterdam. The exhibition, which opened on August 1st 1919, was an enormous success. Half a million people attended, of which some 4,000 received their aerial baptism. When ELTA ended, Fokker took over the field and the halls and established his Netherlands Aircraft Factory there. He also hired the buildings belonging to the Navy Air Department (MLD) at Veere in Zeeland.

STATUTEN

DER

Naamlooze Vennootschap

NEDERLANDSCHE VLIEGTUIGENFABRIEK,

gevestigd te AMSTERDAM.

———

Opgericht bij Akte, den 21 Juli 1919, en gewijzigd bij Akte, den 30

Augustus 1919, ten overstaan van den Notaris F. H. VAN DEN HELM,

te Amsterdam, verleden, op welke akten de Koninklijke Bewilliging

werd verleend bij Besluit van 16 September 1919, No. 27.

"A Dutch Aircraft Company. On the 21st of July inst, the Netherlands Aircraft Factory was founded with as its aims, the manufacture of and the trading in aircraft and fast running vessels and parts thereof, the establishment of flying schools, airfields, landing fields and repair shops, either under own management, or for the account of, or with participation by third parties, and organising flying demonstrations and the exploitation of the transport by air of persons, mail, goods, etc; the taking of aerial photographs for the purpose of exploitation and topographical means, be it for its own account, be it for the account of third parties, or in combination with third parties. The Company Capital amounts Dfl. 1,500,000.00, divided into 50 preferential shares and 1,450 ordinary shares, each of Dfl. 1,000,00, of which 50 preferential and 500 ordinary have been allocated at the time of establishment. Director of the Company is Mr A. H. G. Fokker; Members of the Board are Mr J. B. van Heutz, Mr E. Fokker, C. G. Vattier Kraane, F. H. Fentener van Vlissingen Jr., Mr J. B. van der Hoeven-van Oordt, and Mr D. W. H. Patijn.

We also understand that the Netherlands Automobile and Aircraft Factory Trompenburg Co Ltd is interested in this venture, and will direct its activities solely to the manufacture of automobiles, whilst the current governmental orders will be executed by the new Company.

We have heard that Mr Fokker is making preparations for the construction of a commercial aircraft of a new design, rather than applying himself to the adaption of military aircraft for use in civil capacities by the simple installation of passenger seats, which seems to be the present-day trend."

STATUTES
of the
COMPANY LIMITED
NETHERLANDS AIRCRAFT FACTORY
located in AMSTERDAM.

Established by Act of Law, the 21st of July, and changed by Act of Law on 30th of August, 1919, in the presence of Mr F. H. VAN DEN HELM, Notary, of Amsterdam, for which Acts of Law a Royal Approval was granted as per Decision dated 16th of September, 1919, No. 27.

This seaplane version of the C.I, the C.IW, was built and tested at Schwerin. It was intended for sea-reconnaissance and advanced pilot-training, but only one was produced.

C.I of the Dutch Army Aviation Department (LVA), with blind-flying hood for instrument flying. The aircraft shown was one of those smuggled across the border by Fokker in 1919. The C.I was put into production in Germany in anticipation of an order.

Two-seater cabin of a C.II "passenger" version of the C.I.

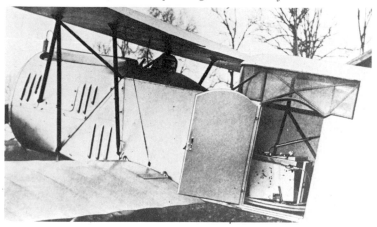

Below: The S.I. was the first real flying training aircraft designed by Platz, accommodating pupil and instructor side-by-side. It was developed from the V.43. The aircraft shown was purchased by the US Army Air Service and designated TW-4.

Bottom of page: A trainload of Fokker aeroplanes at Schwerin. Using trains like this Fokker smuggled 400 engines, 200 aeroplanes and a vast amount of goods into Holland.

The C.II was sold to Holland (KLM), North and South America, and Canada, where it was equipped with skis.

Advertisement of September 6th, 1919, offering ten Rumpler and 237 Fokker single-seat fighters, and monoplanes and biplanes with several seats.

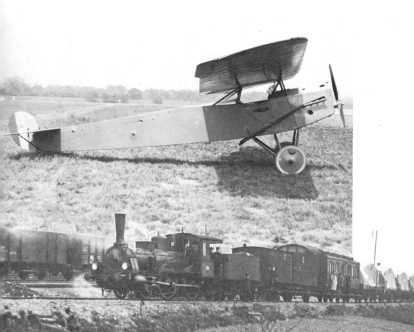

THE AUTO, 9-10-1919

Courage in the Air

August, Amsterdam saw more aircraft in the air in one week, than would normally be seen in a year. There were so many of these giant birds moving above the upturned heads of the good citizens . . . that the novelty soon wore off, and they considered normal that which would have been considered a miracle a few days earlier. After some weeks the "routine" flights were a matter of fact, and the people of Amsterdam, when hearing the rumblings of an engine in the air, would still look up for a while, but no longer until it was out of sight. One looked, interestedly, and said "There goes another one." Watching the flying was now commonplace, the more so because one could fly for 35 guilders. However, one man was capable of repeatedly injecting new life in the waning interest. This was Fokker, the courageous fellow, who even surprised the English officer-pilots accompanying the RAF football team, who called his act "unprecedented". Fokker acrobatted over the stadium; a place which he apparently favoured. Again during the 24-hour cycle races he came, and he then performed some aerobatics over the stadium which drew attention away from the races to such an extent that even the cyclists dropped the pace and changed from performers into audience.

Now Fokker twirled downwards (with the engine switched off) like a sleepy butterfly, and then, when only two to three metres above the ground, the pilot started the engine again; in a second the screw rotated at top speed, pulled, dragged and jolted the aeroplane upwards again, and like a falcon who climbs steeply towards heaven, the monstrous bird reached for the clouds again. And then the loops, fast, and carried out confidently at a height of 100 metres, I ask you! We, the audience, performed the almost traditional act of "holding onto our hats", but Fokker, who handles his aeroplane as if it was a lapdog, rotated his aeroplane in infinite space. It was a joy to watch it.

The stadium management spontaneously put up a "Fokker" premium of 100 guilders which was won by the pair Spears/van Nek, not in the least due to the latter's formidable sprint.

P. Kloppers.

Fokker and his first wife, Elisabeth von Morgen, in conversation with General Snijders and another official during the ELTA exhibition.

Above: Poster for ELTA (First Air Traffic Exhibition Amsterdam), which attracted half a million visitors, 4,000 of whom received their aerial baptism.

Below: The ELTA site at the Johan van Hasselt canal and the Papaverweg in Amsterdam-North. Fokker took over the buildings. Production at Schwerin continued for a while under Platz's supervision. The first Dutch-made Fokker aircraft were manufactured in Veere (see page 50/51).

Fokker with his father.

Fokker with his mother.

Stunting with "the old man".

Having flown for the first time in May 1913 at Houtrust in an automatically stable monoplane flown by Bernard de Waal, the father of the designer Fokker flew with his son from the ELTA site. Mr Fokker senior wrote the following article about these experiences at the request of the editors of the *Haarlems Dagblad* (Haarlem Daily Newspaper) in the August 19th, 1910 number.

Dear Friend,
You asked me to put on paper the impressions one gathers as an "air-passenger". Then read this: My first flight was a peaceful ride in the Fokker used by our Bernard de Waal to fly from Berlin to Soesterberg in one day. Recently he did this excellent flight in 5½ hours. My congratulations. It was very warm, not a whisper of wind. The aeroplane had a difficult take-off and did not rise much (20 to 30 metres): the speed was not very great either. The landing went very smoothly, and when I got out I could say that I'd not had any emotions except at the time that we inclined towards the earth just before landing. This was because I knew that if we come down too hard, first the wheels would break, then the undercarriage and, if the speed is sufficient, the propeller breaks and the machine tips over.

What upset me was the ridiculous wrapping up in a kind of thick fur coat, a cap on my head and a pair of dull celluloid glasses; I even had to put on a thick scarf, so that I only just made it through the manhole and was forced to sit rigidly. Well, I thought, next time I won't have any of these capers. Last Saturday, 9th August, I walked past the ELTA booking office and met my son, who said: "Dad, I heard that you'd like to do a loop, or even several; would you like that today?" I said "That's fine, but can it be soon, because it's almost time to eat, and I like some order in that respect." We went to his flight shed and the engine was checked. One of the mechanics came with coats, glasses etc, and, having learned my lesson, I said "No" to that paraphernalia and would certainly have taken off my own coat if I'd seen a safe place for it. Neither did I want to seem suspicious of the mechanic. I only asked if he was going to throw oil or petrol in my face, and if my new suit would be ruined by accident. The clothing wasn't necessary, he said, so I had plenty of room around me.

As requested I held on tight, although it was not necessary, because loops are made at such a speed that, even when you're upside down, you still feel yourself pressed into the seat. Now I was going to see Amsterdam upside down: I now realise it's the only way to look at it. The engine began to roar faster and faster the aeroplane banked on to a wingtip, changed direction, and we raced towards the cafes at the far end. Long before we got there, the crate jumped into the air as if possessed. Faster

and faster, first this way, then that, as if it were trying to confuse me. It was absolutely successful; I lost all idea of time, speed and direction – sometimes straight on a sudden steep turn to the left, to the right, angled downwards, then I saw the IJ, then ships, rows of houses, the flying park, the Exhibition, the flying field next to the restaurants, a black square which is supposed to be people; whether you are at 250 or at 1,000 metres height, you don't know anything about it; the pilot keeps on looking left and right (there are more crates in the air), suddenly he accelerates, the speed is frightening and whoops . . . you go up and stand on your head, seeing nothing but air. Then you look up to find the earth and you see Amsterdam standing on its head. You look at the ships' decks which are high up in the air, with their masts pointing down, and hanging on to a very thin thread – the IJ – and none of them falls down; the tiles are very firmly fixed so that nothing falls down, or falls towards you. The next second you see Amsterdam make a large sweep and it is on its feet again and you have to look down again to find it. And just when you've found it, whoops, there you are again on your head – a second loop.

It all happens so unbelievably quickly that you can't absorb it. I later heard that loop failed because the engine stopped, and we fell down (backwards or forwards) I had no notion of that. It is as if they're playing catch with you.

At last the aeroplane dived vertically at 50 km/sec, and I wondered how many seconds would pass before we were ground into little bits if an elevator cable broke when trying to lift the nose of the plunging aircraft. It's strange to see the earth rac towards you; suddenly I realised that a full flare-out was happening and that we were racing at uncontrollable speed towards one of the cafes near the bridge to the airfield; the next second we suddenly touched the ground and I thought that we would race straight into the spectators. But no, some distance away we stopped and there was nothing to do but to get out.

Then I heard someone say: "What a beautiful flare-out that was", when I had been thinking that no good at all would come of it.

To have experienced this is priceless. When you do a loop and are standing on your head to look up easily at the world, you have the feeling that you are standing still You do not know whether or not the engine has stopped, but you hear nothing Then suddenly comes that beautiful swing around in which the earth rotates returning to normal again. Now you have to look for the earth beneath you. Some times you lose her.

It is, in a word, so extremely interesting to experience this that the risk to your life is of no consequence. So, once in your life-time, take a trip in the air. You'll never regret it.

Fokker Senior

The bright red converted D.VII used by Fokker for demonstrations and for trips during the ELTA.

Fokker's M.17E, with, behind, left, and, right, the V.36, at the sport aircraft exhibition in 1920.

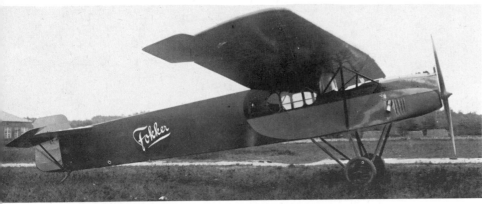

...he F.II prototype in which Bernard de Waal escaped from Schwerin by taking off straight ...it of the hangar. Fokker demonstrated his F.II during KLM's inaugural flight from Amster-...m to London on 17th May 1920, using a converted D.H.9 bomber, and stole the show!

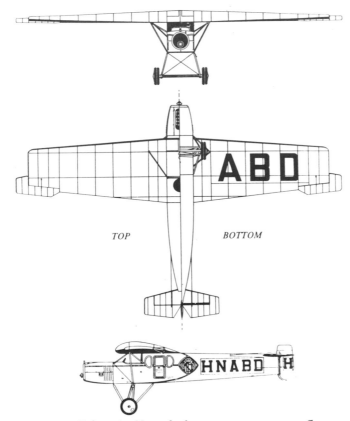

...ree-view drawing of a ...LM F.II. It had a two-...ater cockpit and an ...closed four-passenger ...bin. The payload was ...0kg. Speed: 150 km/hr. ...strong winds the pilots ...metimes flew above ...ains travelling in the ...me direction, so that ...eir passengers would not ...tice that they were mov-...g much slower. The ...nge was 1,200km. 25 to ...0 F.IIs were built; first at ...chwerin and later at ...eere, and the majority ...ere sold to Germany. ...LM ordered two. The ...II was license-built in ...ermany by Grulich.

TOP   BOTTOM

...he F.II prototype under construction at Schwerin. Note the lozenge pattern camouflage on ...e linen tailplane covering. The F.II was the third commercial aeroplane design in the world. ...he first came from Fokker's fellow-countryman, Fritz Koolhoven, and the second from ...unkers.

Immediately after the war Reinhold Platz, in charge of the factory at Schwerin now that Fokker was in Holland, set to work on civil aircraft projects.

Apart from some sports aircraft, he began the construction of a commercial aircraft; the V.44 or F.I. This was a parasol-winged aeroplane with an open cabin. One morning near the almost completed fuselage he found a piece of board bearing the legend: "Faclam's round trips". Faclam was the owner of an open horse-drawn carriage, in which he drove around with pub-crawlers, who were usually drunk.

This made Platz realise that his aircraft was too primitive for modern air traffic, and using the wing of the V.44, the V.45 or F.II was built. It had an enclosed cabin for four passengers and a two-seat cockpit. Fokker ordered that the F.II be flown to Holland to demonstrate it to the newly-formed KLM. However, this was easier said than done, as the export of aircraft from Germany was prohibited.

Bernard de Waal donned a disguise and aided by a few factory-employees, took off directly from the hangar in the F.II leaving the police helpless. When nearly across the border he experienced troubles with his carburettor. Making an emergency landing, he quickly resolved these and took off again, but shortly afterwards he had to make another emergency landing. This time a couple of policemen appeared. De Waal pretended not to know any German and gesticulated to show that he had come from Holland and lost his way.

One policeman left to get instructions. Meanwhile, De Waal convinced the other that it was necessary to test the engine.

The policeman swung the propeller and the engine burst into life. De Waal wasted no time and disappeared, leaving the police-man angrily shaking a fist at him. After one last emergency landing in Holland, he reached Amsterdam by boat.

Shortly after the war the American Lega-tion in The Hague placed an order for C.I scouts and D.VIII fighters. At the end of 1920, Fokker left for the USA on a fact-finding trip, where he was received enthusiastically.

The Army Air Corps arranged an air-tour for him, and this led to the founding of the Netherlands Aircraft Manufacturing Com-pany of Amsterdam in New York, headed by Bob Noorduyn, later to found his own Company.

The Fokker factory at Veere, alongside the Walcheren Canal. In the summer of 1921 Platz and his staff moved from Schwerin to Veere. The great distance from the parent-factory in Amsterdam incurred high expenditure and the testing of land-planes from the military field at Souburg also met with problems. The move to Amsterdam began in October 1924, but the factory remained in use until July 1926.

A T.II bomber on wooden floats. With a crew of three and a 400 h.p. Liberty engine the speed was 152 km/hr and the range 650 km. Three T.IIs were delivered to the US Navy.

The T.IIIW bomber for the Portuguese Navy was, like the T.II, built at Veere. It was a larger version of the T.II and had a 360 h.p. Rolls-Royce Eagle or Napier Lion engine. Five T.IIIWs were produced.

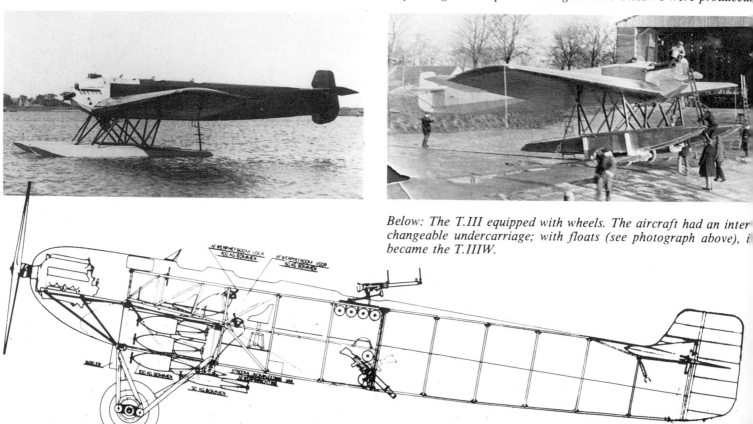

Below: The T.III equipped with wheels. The aircraft had an interchangeable undercarriage; with floats (see photograph above), it became the T.IIIW.

The first F.III, named after Henry Hudson's "Halve Maen" (Half Moon), was demonstrated in America by Bert Acosta in the summer of 1921. The aircraft was a revelation to the Americans, but the country was too far behind in civil aviation to purchase a sophisticated aircraft of this type.

During the winter of 1920-21 KLM ceased flying. On April 14th, 1921, flights were resumed with a new type of Fokker aircraft, the F.III. The wider, shorter fuselage could accommodate five passengers in a cabin of Victorian appearance. The pilot sat beside the engine in an open cockpit, being roasted on one side, and frozen to death on the other, and during rainy weather the water poured in over the small screen so that he was afloat on his hardwood seat.

The "heating" for the passengers, which, unfortunately, also functioned in the summer, produced a frightful stench. This, coupled with the bumps due to low flying, frequently caused air-sickness. The passengers were given an aluminium tray with a lid, later replaced by the now ubiquitous paper bag which could be thrown out of the window.

In spite of these short-comings, the F.III was the aircraft on which KLM founded its reputation. When other companies' aircraft were grounded by bad weather conditions, KLM's F.IIIs kept on flying. The F.IIIs also flew in Germany, Russia and Hungary.

The German Aero Lloyd company manufactured a number of modified F.IIIs under the supervision of Ing Grulich.

Above: The F.III seaplane version of the F.III.

The F.III was also demonstrated in the USA, but although everyone was impressed, the time was not yet ripe in that country for commercial air traffic. The F.III was exhibited at the 1921 Paris Air Show where its stand had to be guarded by six policemen, when the French public discovered that this product of the Netherlands Aircraft Factories was a Fokker. Fokker himself also had to be protected. In the summer of 1921 Platz and his staff moved from Schwerin to Veere, in the province of Zeeland, where Fokker had rented a shed from the Naval Air Service. Some F.IIs were produced there and the last series of F.IIIs, which had been started at Schwerin, was completed at this location.

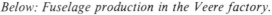

Below: Fuselage production in the Veere factory.

The F.IV, F.V, F.VI and the first F.VII, dealt with on the following pages, were also produced at Veere, as were the three T.II torpedo-carrying aircraft for the US Navy and five T.III torpedo-carrying aircraft for Portugal. The factory at Veere was in use until 1926, during which period the S.II and S.III trainers, the FG.I and the FG.II gliders, and the fuselages for the Russian C.I, D.XI and D.XIII aircraft were produced there.

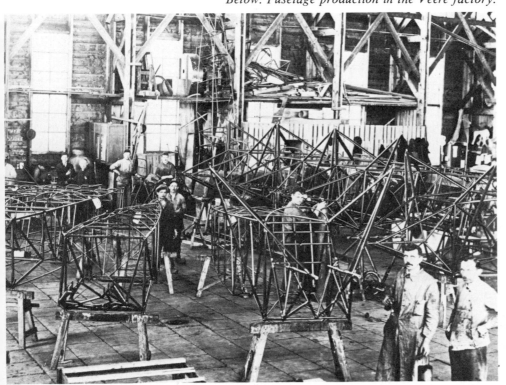

Anthony Fokker in the cockpit of an F.III. This photograph clearly shows the position of the pilot next to the engine. On one side he was fried, whilst on the other he froze. Only once was a pilot enthusiastic about this position. That was when a throttle-lever came loose and he was able to control the carburettor directly by hand.

ROYAL·DUTCH·AIR·SERVICE·C.

THE FLYING DUTCHMAN

FICTION BECOMES **FACT**

A KLM poster of 1924. The pilot points out his F.III – which he has apparently abandoned for that purpose – to the skipper of the legendary ghost-ship, Joost van der Decken.

Advertisement in The Aeroplane *of March 22nd, 1922.*

Why pay the

EXCESSIVE PRICES

some Aircraft Manufacturers are asking for their machines

if you can get an up-to-date

"FOKKER"

at <u>half</u> the money?

"Fokker - Limousine FIII" with 360 h p. "Rolls-Royce" engine.

paying load 800 Kg.

For further information apply to:

N. V. NEDERLANDSCHE VLIEGTUIGENFABRIEK

Rokin 84.   <u>Amsterdam.</u>   Cable Address : Fokplanes

The F.III cabin. The armchairs are anchored to the floor.

52

U.S. Air Service

June, 1923   Price 25 Cents

Vol. 8, No. 6 $3.00 a Year

CONTINENTAL

TRANS~   NUMBER

F. Melville

Fokker Army T2 on flight across continent

Top: Fokker's FG.2 two-seat glider during the Rhön Gliding Competition of 1922.

Above: The single-seat FG.I.

Below: The Fokker F.IV (US Army Air Service designation T-2) in which John A. Macready and Oakley G. Kelly were the first to cross the North-American Continent from coast-to-coast on May 2 and 3, 1922. A sister-aeroplane was modified to an Ambulance aircraft, with the designation A-2.

Petrol and oil for the coast-to-coast flight, left: Macready, right: Kelly.

Frontispiece of the magazine US Air Service of June 1923.

In 1922 Fokker's name appeared in all the American newspapers. Lieutenants John A. Macready and Oakley G. Kelly were the first to fly non-stop across the American Continent on 2 and 3 May, using a Fokker F.IV. In the summer of 1922 Fokker visited America for the second time, and decided to establish a factory there. This meant taking a great risk unless he had firm orders, but General "Billy" Mitchell was to pave the way for him.

He had recently visited the Dutch Fokker factory and also the Aviation Department. He asked the Technical Manager of the Aviation Department, Mr Stephan, to draft a memorandum concerning the manufacture and maintenance of aircraft constructed of welded steel tubing. Mitchell used this memorandum in a report for the Army Air Service, which in 1924 resulted in an order for the construction of 100 D.H.-4 bombers, and later for another 35.

Fokker also made the headlines in another sphere in 1922. In August he participated in the Rhön gliding competition with his FG.I and FG.II, single- and two-seat gliders. At the start he made a few modest hops, but it soon became obvious that this type of flying was no problem to him either. With the FG.II he made the first passenger-carrying glider flight in the world.

In October he took part in a glider meeting, organised by the *Daily Mail*. Some days earlier he moved into the hotel "Peace Haven", not far from Newhaven on the Channel, where the meeting was to be held. To start with he gave a demonstration, which, though simple, led the British press to acclaim him as the first glider pilot over England. This was untrue, because Percy Pilcher had experimented with his homemade hang gliders in the late 1800s.

On October 16th the meeting started. The first pilot made flights varying between 1min 58sec to 3min. Most of the competitors understood little about gliding and flew straight down to the valley. Fokker however, flew along the ridge, and using thermals, achieved a time of 7min with a *Daily Mail* reporter as a passenger.

At the end of the day he remained airborne for 37min 6sec. The other participants had been observing Fokker closely and now achieved better times, but Fokker had stolen the show again. *The Aeroplane* wrote: "Mr Fokker shows how."

B.I Flying Boat designed by Rethel at Veere. One aircraft was delivered to the Navy Air Service and used in the Dutch East Indies.

This Spanish C.III was, in fact, a C.I with an Hispano-Suiza engine. The C.IIIs were used for advanced training.

Fokker F.VI (PW-5). The designation F.VI was rather curious as it concerns a fighter, while the letter "F" was used by Fokker to designate commercial aircraft. In this case the "F" most probably stood for "Fighter". The F.VI was developed from the V.37. Two aircraft designated V.40, with Wright-Hispano engines and two Browning machine guns, were supplied to the US Army Air Service in 1922. These aircraft had no type-designations. They were followed by 10 PW-5s, the USAAS designation of the F.VI. Maximum speed 230 km/hr. One of the V.40s, A.S.64231, crashed due to flutter on March 13th, 1922.

D.IX (PW-6) of the US Army Air Service. One of Fokker's first post-war fighter designs, it was developed from the D.VII and was very similar. The prototype had a streamlined fuel tank built around the wheel axle, (like the C.I), but this tank was later removed upon delivery as PW-6 to the US Army Air Services. Only one was built. The aircraft had a Wright-Hispano engine of 300 h.p. and was armed with two machine guns. Maximum speed was 220 km/hr.

S.II Trainer with adjacent seats for pupil and tutor. The aircraft was fitted successively with Thulin, Oberursel and Curtiss engines. The Aviation Department purchased 15 S.IIs with the registration numbers 84 to 98.

An S.IIA Ambulance aircraft. This one was an S.II, modified at Soesterberg Airfield, the open space between the top wing and fuselage top surface being covered in with transparent panels. The patient lay on a stretcher with his legs towards the tailplane.

The F.V as a monoplane.

The F.V as a biplane.

The Fokker F.V was designed to meet the demand for increased capacity. The F.III was increasingly unable to cope with growing air traffic, and the F.IV was too large. The F.V accommodated eight passengers and two pilots. More attention was paid to passenger comfort, and a separate space was provided for luggage. Another great improvement was the provision of a toilet. The aircraft could be used as a monoplane or as a biplane; as a monoplane the F.V, with an all-up weight of 2.655 kg, could reach a speed of 192 km/hr, while as a biplane the speed was 180 km/hr with a total weight of 3,134 kg. The prototype was tested by the German-Russian Aviation Company, Deruluft, but was not satisfactory, and spent its life in the service of a small Austrian company.

Right: Left to right, Holland's first aviation journalist, Henri Hegener, Friedrich Seekatz, Head of Fokker's sales department and Cis van Rhijn, Fokker's secretary, in the F.V cabin en route *to Moscow. Journalist Hegener was not allowed to enter by the Russians, and had to get out in Berlin.*

In the winter of 1922/23 Reinhold Platz designed and constructed a glider. The idea occurred during a sailing trip on the Schelde. To a certain extent sailing on water can be compared (aerodynamically) with gliding. After several tests with small and large models, Platz constructed a full-size glider. Its fuselage comprised a curved steel tube with a circular-section wooden beam inserted through it at the rear. The wing spars were two wooden masts which were inserted into two receptacles welded to the fuselage tube near the pilot's seat.

The "main sail", or wing, was attached to these two masts. The two separate forward jibs were attached to jib-masts, which could be moved by the pilot simultaneously or separately as required. By moving the two jibs up or down, longitudinal control was obtained. By moving one jib up and the other down, lateral control was possible.

Platz's glider had a wing span of 6.60 metres and weighed 40kg. It could be assembled by one man within 15min, and dismantled within 10min. As shown below, it could be transported on a bicycle. After some 50 unmanned test flights, piloted trials were made. The photograph below shows one of the first manned trials, when ropes were used to restrain the craft. The control-system appeared easy to operate.

This light B.II reconnaissance seaplane made its maiden flight on December 15th, 1923. With its Rolls-Royce Eagle VIII engine of 360 h.p. a cruising speed of 175 km/hr. was reached. The B.II could be operated from warships, and one example was tested by the Naval Air Service.

Unlike the S.II, the S.III trainer had the seats in tandem again. The Naval Air Service bought 18 of these aircraft and built one themselves. Two were sold to the Danish Air Force. Many Dutch naval pilots received their primary training in the S.III; "a kite you could use for reading and writing."

The D.X was developed at Schwerin from the V.41, and was partly finished when Platz moved to Veere with his staff. The aeroplane was completed there in 1919 as the prototype for the D.X. In 1923 Spain purchased ten production aircraft. Its engine was a 300 h.p. Hispano-Suiza and its speed 255 km/hr.

D.XI fighter of the Swiss Air Force. Altogether 117 D.XIs were built for the Argentine, Rumania, Russia, Spain, the USA and Switzerland.

D.XI fighters in production for Russia. The Russian inspectors became increasingly unpleasant, and finally, access to the factory was forbidden to them.

The D.XII was a development of the D.IX. The expected orders from the USA did not materialise, and only three were built.

The prototype of the DC.I, which Grasé demonstrated at Gothenborg. The DC.I was a fighter-version of the popular C.IV, with a shorter-span wing. Grasé also demonstrated the DC.I in Spain with much success.

The Prototype C.IV with a 400 h.p. Liberty engine. The C.IV was built as a successor to the C.I, being more spacious and able to transport more equipment. The C.IVA fighter-scout had less wing span, whilst the C.IVB and the C.IVC scouts had a greater span. Fokker manufactured 139 C.IVs and a number were also built in Spain.

The C.IV was a float-plane. In the machine depicted the Argentinian Major Zanni flew from Amsterdam to Tokyo in 1924. The C.IV was a great success, and was used in America (where it was known as the CO-4), the Argentine, Italy, Holland and the Dutch East Indies, Russia and Spain.

The year 1923 was again noteworthy for the large orders received by the Fokker factory. At this period Russia was one of the most important customers. They had earlier purchased 92 D.VII and C.I aircraft, and now ordered 125 D.XI fighters. In 1924 some 55 C.IVs were added. These orders, however, were not free from problems. A Russian delegation, headed by comrade Poscholkoff, was sent to the Amsterdam factory to inspect everything and, fearing for their future in Russia if they overlooked a deficiency, they became more and more irritating, even interfering with production. Finally they were forbidden to enter the factory. Later they were accused of making political propaganda, and were requested to leave the country. The Russian order was then inspected by Dutchmen.

In that same period Fokker was asked by Seekatz to go to Hamburg in connection with an important order. It concerned 50 D.XI and 50 D.XII fighter aircraft for the Argentine. Hugo Stinnes, a millionaire, acted as intermediary. It appeared, however, that the order was not what it seemed. The 50 D.XIIIs (the 50 D.XIs were cancelled) were delivered to Lipetzk, near Moscow in Russia, where a secret German flying school was established. Between 1925 and 1933 about 120 fighter pilots and observers were trained there. Fokker also met with success in Spain, where the DC.I, a C.IV derivative, was well-demonstrated by Mr Grasé and won the competition against French, English and German-Italian entrants. The C.IV was built in Madrid by Jorge Loring, under license from Fokker.

In 1923 KLM flew its Fokker F.IIIs with a regularity never equalled by any other aviation company. The F.IIIs operated by the German-Russian company Deruluft also performed satisfactorily.

During the International Aviation Exhibition and Flying Week at Gothenborg, Sweden, Fokker won the stunt-flying competition, and Grasé came second in the Rotterdam-Gothenborg race, flying a DC.I Lieutenant Versteegh of the Aviation Department, together with Lieutenants van Weerden-Poelman and Jongbloed and Sergeants van de Griend and Bakkenes, flying D.VIIs, gave such a perfect demonstration of formation flying that a Swedish newspaper wrote: "They flew as the five fingers of one hand."

Above: Captain Versteegh (nicknamed "Flying Daddy Versteegh") and his men being fêted upon their return from Gothenborg. Together with van Weerden-Poelman, Jongbloed, van de Griend and Bakkenes, Versteegh gave an unparalleled formation-flying demonstration. A Swedish journalist wrote: "They flew as five fingers of one hand." From that day, the Versteegh flight was called "The five fingers" (photograph, top left).

Above: "The five fingers" in formation. The front, light-grey two-seat D.VII was a personal present from Fokker to Versteegh. The other aircraft were normal D.VIIs.

Right: In the 'twenties the S.IV was the basic primary trainer of the Aviation Department, and many famous Dutch pilots received their first lessons in it. The S.IV was a development of the S.III equipped with an air-cooled engine, as these were more easily obtained in the 110 to 130 h.p. range than the liquid-cooled engines. The Aviation Department purchased 30 aircraft, which at first were fitted with 125 h.p. Le Rhône-Oberursel engines (bottom picture). In 1926-1927 these were replaced by 148 h.p. Armstrong-Siddeley Mongoose engines (above).

VISIT BY THE ROYAL FAMILY TO THE NETHERLANDS AIRCRAFT FACTORY

From the *Fokker Bulletin* of April/May 1924

On the afternoon of April 3rd, 1924, HM the Queen Wilhelmina, accompanied by HRH Prince Hendrik and Princess Juliana, paid an official visit to the Netherlands Aircraft Factories in Amsterdam.

The Royal Family and escort arrived through the gaily-decorated streets of Amsterdam, and then went by boat across the IJ to the factory, where they were received by the directors and wholeheartedly cheered by 1,500 employees.

HM spent a long time in the various workshops. Particular interest was paid to the new, large F.VII passenger monoplane, which would shortly replace the F.III aircraft on the air-routes to London, Paris, Copenhagen, etc. The Royal guests viewed the interior of the cosy cabin, and Princess Juliana and her friend Princess von Erbach were seated in the two pilot's seats whilst the aircraft's flight control system was explained to them.

Mr H. (Bertus) Grasé M.Sc., was born in 1891. After his studies he worked for the Governmental Research Service for Aviation, the predecessor of the present-day NLR (National Air and Space Laboratory). Not only was he a very good technician, but he was also an excellent pilot, and his demonstrations at Gothenborg and Madrid earned him much fame. He later modernised the Fokker F.VII, and the resulting aircraft, the F.VIIA, was a faster, lighter and more manoeuvrable aircraft. In 1925 he broke four world records in the Fokker D.XIII. Grasé died on August 27th, 1929.

Below: The D.XIII, with its 260 km/hr, was the fastest fighter in the world. This picture shows a German D.XIII which operated from Lipetzk in Russia.

Below: The C.V-A, the prototype of the successful C.V series.

Bottom of page: D.XIIIs of the "Stinnes" order.

Fokker saying goodbye to van der Hoop prior to his departure for the Dutch East Indies in H-NACC. On the left is Albert Plesman.

On October 1st the F.VII prototype, H-NACC, with van der Hoop, van Weerden Poelman and van der Broeke as its crew, left Schiphol *en route* for the Dutch East Indies. A few days later the aircraft made an emergency landing at Philippopel due to a cooler defect. The right wheel broke off and the wing tip struck the ground. This seemed to mark a premature end to the flight, but after a few days the glad tidings arrived that the weekly magazine *Het Leven* had put up 12.000 guilders for a new engine. The journey was continued on November 3rd, and Batavia (now Jakarta) was reached on November 24th. H-NACC was sent home by ship, and the crew, after a sea-journey to Marseilles, flew home in another F.VII, H-NACK. Their reception in Holland was tumultuous.

The engine which the weekly magazine Het Leven (Life) donated, en route by means of 1 h.p.

A close-up of the Rolls-Royce Eagle engine, cockpit and the shock-absorbing main leg, fitted with rubber rings, of the F.VII. The pilot was still accommodated in an open cockpit.

The cabin of the F.VII with a view into the cockpit. The cabin was notably more spacious than that of the F.III, and had eight seats.

Right: The F.VII's instrument panel. Far right: The F.VII was the first KLM aircraft with a toilet installed.

DE TELEGRAAF

The flight has been accomplished.

Amsterdam-Batavia: 15,000km.

A VICTORIOUS JOURNEY TO THE FINISH.

"You are men of courage and bravery, like the pioneers at the end of the 15th century", said the Governor-General Mr Fock . . . The crowd is delirious with excitement and carries the flyers four times around the field.

LANDED!

Weltevreden, 24th November. The Fokker aircraft has landed safely at 1.20 p.m. (Batavia-time) – (Aneta). The pilot is in shirt-sleeves, and without paying much attention to the thunderous ovations, checks his aircraft calmly. Tien van Weerden Poelman comes out of the cabin.

Van der Hoop stays inside for a short while to arrange a few details. The public can hardly be restrained, and pushes forward continually. Finally some members of the press fetch van der Hoop, and accompany him to the front of the grandstand of the Governor-General. The latter then makes a speech, stating that the East-Indian Government and HM the Queen . . .

In April this year one of the most important commercial aircraft in the world made its maiden flight. The F.VII and its derivatives were to revolutionise air transport. Slowly, but steadily, the F.III's capacity had become inadequate for the rapidly-expanding air traffic, and KLM in particular was pushing for a larger successor. On December 10th, 1923, KLM signed a temporary contract for three F.VIIs, with an option on another three later on. The order would be confirmed if the prototype proved satisfactory during practical use. In 1924 the first F.VII went into service with KLM. Ever since the end of World War One plans had existed for a flight to the Dutch East Indies, and during the design of the F.VII the requirements for such a flight had been taken into account. In particular, the undercarriage was strongly constructed to allow for the bad landing fields expected along the route.

The F.VII had a Rolls-Royce Eagle engine, and its cabin could accommodate eight passengers. A separate luggage compartment was provided, and also a toilet, so that passengers no longer had to spend long hours with their legs crossed.

Fokker rented the Witteman-Lewis aircraft factory at Teterboro, together with the adjoining airfield at Hasbrouck Heights, New Jersey, USA. In May 1924 a new company was formed, the Atlantic Corporation, with Lorillard Spencer as President and Robert B. C. Noorduyn as General Manager. In the same year Fokker received an order to replace 100 de Havilland D.H.4 fuselages by welded steel units, and simultaneously, 35 new aircraft were ordered from him. In Buenos Aires, Captain Ballod, flying a Fokker C.IV broke the world altitude record with a payload. A plan by the Portuguese pilot Sacadura Cabral to fly around the world with a Fokker T.III was not fulfilled. In November, while delivering a T.IIIW, he vanished without trace in a dense fog off the Belgian coast. Another sad event was the death of Fokker's father on December 20th.

A C.VC of the Naval Air Service, who ordered six. They could be fitted with wheels or floats as required.

C.VW seaplane. Though the type proved unsatisfactory in Holland, Sweden converted C.Vs into seaplanes and were very satisfied with them.

The D.XIV was a very advanced monoplane fighter. The prototype crashed before all of its initial design problems were solved.

The first American Fokker design was the Universal. The brainchild of Noorduyn, it was a great commercial success.

The F.VII used by Fokker during demonstrations in England. This aircraft had a Napier Lion engine installed.

The wheel undercarriage of the Universal was interchangeable with floats or skis, a feature which made it very popular in Canada and the USA.

A Fokker D.XIII and a Spin at the Paris Air Show.

Left: Fokker conversing with the Director of the Napier engine factory. In the centre is Fokker's co-director, Stephan.

FOKKER AIR TRAFFIC 1925.

THE FOLLOWING STATISTICS ARE BASED ON THE RESULTS OF COMPANIES OPERATING WITH FOKKER MACHINES.

ROYAL DUTCH AIR SERVICE (K.L.M.)

PASSENGERS	1924	6.157	
"	1925		10.912
FREIGHT AND MAIL	1924	156.970 Kilos	
" "	1925		354.182 Kilos
DISTANCE FLOWN	1924	789.615 Kms.	
" "	1925		1.103.895 Kms.

DEUTSCHER AERO LLOYD.

PASSENGERS	1924	1.749	
"	1925		17.421
FREIGHT AND MAIL	1924	19.803 Kilos	
" "	1925	144.662 Kilos	
DISTANCE FLOWN	1924	265.300 Kms.	
" "	1925		1.352.757 Kms.

RUSSO-GERMAN AIR TRAFFIC CO (DERULUFT)

PASSENGERS	1924	522
"	1925	1.733
FREIGHT AND MAIL	1924	34.454 Kilos
" " "	1925	64.827 Kilos
DISTANCE FLOWN	1924	334.000 Kms.
" "	1925	470.487 Kms.

HUNGARIAN AIR TRAFFIC CO.

1924	1.532	
1925	2.549	
1924	27.572	Kilos
1925	68.129	Kilos
1924	90.765	Kms.
1925	116.231	Kms.

SUEDDEUTSCHER AERO LLOYD.

PASSENGERS MAY 1 - DEC. 31	1925		10.750
FREIGHT AND MAIL MAY 1 - DEC. 31	1925	27.302 Kilos	
DISTANCE FLOWN MAY 1 - DEC. 31	1925	276.597 Kms.	

IN ADDITION TO THE ABOVE, OTHER PROMINENT COMPANIES HAVE A NUMBER OF FOKKER MACHINES IN THEIR FLEET.

OUR LATEST TYPE "FOOLPROOF" COMMERCIAL MACHINE, THE THREE-ENGINED FVII-3M, DESIGNED AND BUILT DURING 1925, PARTICIPATED IN THE "FORD RELIABILITY TOUR", WHICH IT FINISHED FIRST, HAVING GAINED A "PERFECT SCORE" ON EACH LEG OF THE COURSE, NOTWITHSTANDING VERY UNFAVORABLE WEATHER CONDITIONS. THE SAME MACHINE WAS USED BY COMMANDER RICHARD E. BYRD ON HIS MEMORABLE FLIGHT TO THE NORTH POLE AND BACK ON MAY 9, 1926.

FOKKER COMMERCIAL AEROPLANES HAVE FLOWN IN REGULAR AIR SERVICE A DISTANCE EQUAL TO OVER TWO HUNDRED TIMES ROUND THE WORLD.

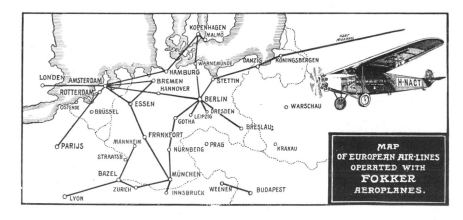

Details of the European routes flown by Fokker aircraft in 1925.

On April 15th, 1925, Fokker demonstrated the F.VII in England. It was an extremely stable aircraft with a very low stalling speed, and the magazine *The Aeroplane* had already pointed out several times that Fokker aircraft were an exception to the rule, as many of the commercial aircraft of the day had nasty low-speed characteristics. The demonstration was a great success. Both observers and passengers held their breath when Fokker pulled the stick back until all forward speed had been lost, but instead of dropping a wing and entering into a spin, the F.VII calmly pointed its nose downwards to pick up speed. *Flight* devoted six pages to this demonstration. However, there was still room for improvement in the F.VII. Grasé was given a free hand by Fokker, and modified some items. The wing tips were rounded and the ailerons were moved inboard from the wing tips. Mr Roosenschoon greatly simplified the undercarriage. The improved version was designated F.VIIA, and was 22 km/hr faster than the F.VII and more manoeuvrable.

In May Fokker visited America for the fourth time. Conditions now seemed better for the sale of long-distance commercial aircraft, and Henry Ford, the car-king, offered him the opportunity to demonstrate his aircraft. To stimulate the public's interest in aviation, Ford organised a 1,500-mile "Reliability Tour", and Fokker decided to participate in a three-engined aircraft.

Early in July he cabled Platz in Amsterdam to say that a three-engined F.VII was to be built. Platz executed this order in eight weeks. To avoid extra testing and design, he suspended the additional engines beneath the wing of an F.VIIA. After a demonstration for KLM, the F.VIIA/3m, as it was later called, was shipped to the USA, where Fokker flew the aircraft from New York to Detroit on September 26th. The "Ford Reliability Tour" was such a triumph for Fokker, that the magazine *Aviation* reported on the "Fokker Publicity Tour". On every leg of the tour, Fokker came in first, then made local trips with the press to pass the time until the other competitors had landed. Consequently, most of the news and photographic coverage had Fokker's aircraft as their subject. In the summer of 1925 Fokker settled permanently in America. In May the Fokker company sold the 50 D.XI fighters, previously cancelled from the Stinnes order, to Rumania.

A little later Bertus Grasé broke four world speed records with the D.XIII fighter.

Two newspaper cuttings of 1925.

Fokker demonstrates near London.
Today Reuter wired: A demonstration of the latest development in aviation was today carried out at Croydon, in the presence of representatives of the Ministry of Aviation. Two aircraft, namely one ten-seat Fokker and a single-seat Avro, carried out some tests to prove that if an aircraft dived owing to lack of airspeed, the pilot could maintain control, so that it only lost a little height. Fokker states that the aircraft will not nose-over on losing airspeed, even if the pilot fails to correct. Sefton Brancker, Director of Civil Aviation, flew with Fokker, and – after the flight – stated that in his opinion the new construction represented a big advance in aviation, and that about 50 per cent of the accidents now occurring would not take place.

THE WORLD RECORDS BY GRASÉ
The Hague, 25th July 1925. Recently, Mr B. Grasé of the Netherlands Aircraft Factory Fokker, flying a Fokker Napier D.XIII Aircraft, established four speed records over 100 and 200km with payloads of 250kg and 500kg which have been recognised by the FAI. The speeds attained were – over 100km – 266.6 003km/hr, and over 200km – 265 km/hr.

65

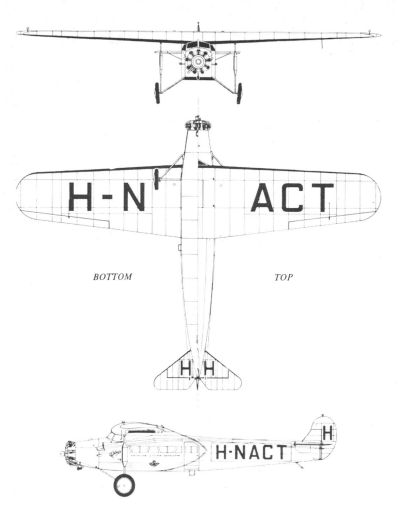

BOTTOM   TOP

The F.VIIA prototype. Compare the improved wing and undercarriage with that of the F.VII on page 63.

In America Fokker demonstrated an F.VIIA equipped with a Hornet engine. He had intended to have the single-engined F.VIIA participate in the Ford Reliability Tour alongside the F.VIIIA/3m, but engine failure forced him to make an emergency landing en route to Detroit.

Three-view drawing of the F.VIIA H-NACT, the first of the type for KLM. The aircraft was in use until May 10th, 1940, when German bombers blew it to pieces. The F.VIIA masquerading as H-NACT in the Aviation Museum "Aviodome" at Schiphol Airport was purchased in Denmark.

Below: Construction of an F.VIIA wing. Fokker's formula for success in the 'twenties and at the beginning of the 'thirties was a wooden wing. The fuselage and tailplane were of welded tubular steel construction, covered with linen. In the second half of the 'thirties all-metal constructions came into use.

The first three-engined F.VII: "Trimotor".

Newspaper Cuttings concerning the "Ford Reliability Tour".

The three-engined Fokker Aircraft in America.

As already stated on the occasion of the demonstration of the three-engined Fokker aircraft at Schiphol on the 7th inst, this aircraft was specially designed for America, where a three-engined aircraft is required for the long distances between the major cities, and in particular for the nightly mail-flights.

On the 29th inst. we were cabled from Chicago that the aircraft had arrived in New York on the 21st. After disembarking and assembly, it was able to leave on the 26th to take part in the "Commercial Reliability Tour", which commenced at Detroit. This race was organised by the well-known car manufacturer, Ford, and his son, Edsel B. Ford. The latter is much interested in aviation. The tour is intended to show the possibilities of air transport, and the "Ford Trophy", donated by Edsel Ford, is a challenge trophy, so that every year the manufacturers of commercial aircraft may enter the race. Government-owned aircraft cannot enter for the Tour. The aircraft must meet certain structural requirements concerning loadings, capacity and safety factors.

The different stages to be flown in the race (held for the first time this year) are:

28th Sept: Detroit-Fort Wayne-Chicago
29th Sept: Chicago-Iowa City-Omaha
30th Sept: Omaha-St Joseph-Kansas City
1st Oct: Kansas City-St Louis
2nd Oct: St Louis-Indianapolis-Columbus
3rd Oct: Columbus-Cleveland-Detroit

Upon the arrival of Mr Fokker and his three-engined aircraft at Detroit, after a flight from New York via Buffalo, it appeared that great interest in the aircraft had been aroused. Henry Ford and his son, Edsel, viewed the aircraft, and Mr Fokker explained everything.

Yesterday the aircraft started in the race for the Ford Trophy. It flew the first stage as given above, and arrived in Chicago.

The Hague Aneta office reports:- Following the previous message concerning participation of the three-engined Fokker aircraft in the race for the Ford Trophy, the following can be added: The Fokker also came first in both legs of the second stage to Omaha on the second day.

The three-engined Fokker Aircraft in America

A cable from Kansas City to The Hague Aneta office states:-

The three-engined Fokker aircraft taking part in the Ford Trophy Tour arrived here after flying the two legs of the third day. The aircraft was well ahead of the other participants flying Stout, Curtiss and Junkers aircraft.

Two thunderstorms were flown through, and the Fokker carried a load of almost 1,400kg which included nine passengers. The Tour is continuing today.

The Fight for the Ford Trophy

A cable to Aneta in The Hague from St Louis states: The three-engined Fokker participating in the race for the Ford Trophy has arrived in St Louis, having flown the stage of the fourth day.

THE FOKKER VII IN AMERICA
(by our correspondent)

New York, 2 Oct. – The F.VII has today safely made the long flight from St Louis (1,125 miles).

Up to now the Ford all-metal Stout monoplane has the highest average speed, i.e. $100\frac{1}{10}$ m.p.h. Then follows the Fokker F.VIII at $99\frac{1}{10}$ m.p.h.; third is Casey Jones (who had to carry out repairs in Omaha), with $98\frac{1}{2}$ m.p.h.; fourth the Mercury, $90\frac{1}{2}$ m.p.h.

On Friday they shall fly to Indianapolis and Columbus, and on Saturday to Cleveland and Detroit.

THE FORD TROPHY TOUR

St Louis, 2 Oct. – The three-engined Fokker aircraft taking part in the Ford Trophy Tour has arrived safely after flying the fourth day's stage – (Aneta).

The last laps of the Ford Trophy Tour

A cable dated Oct 3rd from Indianapolis to The Hague office of Aneta states:

Mr Fokker has arrived here with his three-engined Fokker aircraft in the Ford Trophy Tour, after the start in St Louis had been delayed for three hours owing to fog.

The Tour continues today with the last two stretches, so that the aircraft will reach the finish at Detroit this afternoon or evening.

The Commercial Airplane Reliability Tour for the Ford Trophy is, as the name indicates, not a race, but a reliability competition. The aircraft must carry a load of half an English pound per cubic inch of engine volume. They must fly at an average speed of 80 m.p.h.. To gain the required number of points all stretches must be flown, 70 per cent of them at a minimum speed not less than 30 per cent of the aforementioned speed, whilst the flight time must not be more than 50 per cent of the time relative to that speed.

The three engines of the Fokker F.VII have not exceeded 1,400 r.p.m. during this Tour (the maximum r.p.m. for Wright engines is 1,800). In this cruising regime the Fokker reaches an average speed of 98 m.p.h. The Ford Stout aircraft is continually flying at full engine power, and so reaches a speed of 101 m.p.h. To date the Fokker has achieved a perfect score for each leg of the Tour, i.e., it has obtained the points as described above. The Fokker carries two pilots, seven passengers and about 220kg as ballast, as well as 715 litres of fuel at take-off.

Fokker wins the Ford Trophy

A cable from Detroit to the Aneta office in The Hague:

Having flown the last leg perfectly in his three-engined aircraft, Mr Fokker has come first in the Ford Reliability Tour, after flying 3,400km in six days. Upon arrival, during a heavy thunderstorm, a camera fell from the luggage rack on to Mr Fokker's head. He suffered some light contusions, but was otherwise uninjured.

The tour was a perfect success for the three-engined, ten-passenger Fokker aeroplane.

The three-engined Fokker aircraft in America.

A cable from New York to the Aneta office in The Hague:

Fokker has flown back to New York in the three-engined aircraft which so successfully participated in the Ford Trophy Tour. The 4,800km flight was made without interruption.

Fokker's Trimotor next to a Douglas World Cruiser in a hangar during the Ford Reliability Tour.

Top: *The first three-engined Fokker, the F.VIIA/3m, in which Fokker was so successful during the Ford Reliability Tour, was made available by Mr Edsel Ford to Lt Cdr Richard Byrd, who used it to become the first man to fly across the North Pole. Although Ford owned the aircraft and Byrd made the flight, the name FOKKER was painted so prominently on the aircraft that Byrd must have thought he was advertising for Fokker. The latter had foreseen the importance of the flight and its publicity value, and had, therefore, stipulated in the sales contract that the name "Fokker" was to be displayed conspicuously on wing and fuselage.*

Right: *Byrd (right) and the* Josephine Ford, *which was named after Edsel Ford's youngest daughter. In the last months of 1926 the* Josephine Ford *made a propaganda tour through America, sponsored by the Daniel Guggenheim Aviation Foundation, before it found its final resting place in the Henry Ford Museum.*

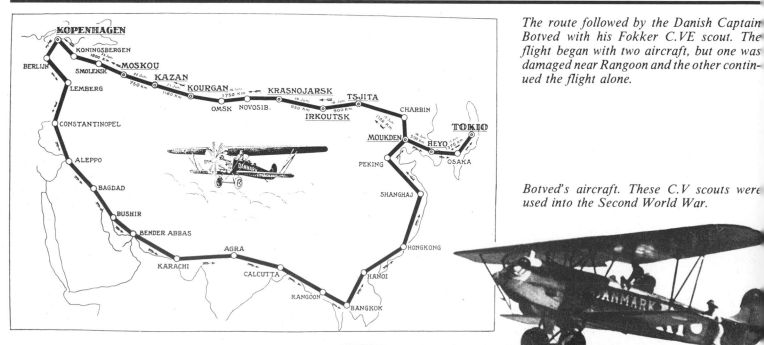

The route followed by the Danish Captain Botved with his Fokker C.VE scout. The flight began with two aircraft, but one was damaged near Rangoon and the other continued the flight alone.

Botved's aircraft. These C.V scouts were used into the Second World War.

A C.VD of the Aviation Department, with a 450 h.p. Hispano engine. Another version of this aircraft, designated C.VI, had a 350 h.p. Hispano engine.

This C.V was imported by the Japanese Army for evaluation.

This F.VIIA/3m was purchased by the British Air Ministry for evaluation. It was later fitted with a Monospar wing.

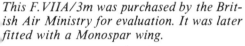

Below: F.VIIA in which Grasé flew from Rotterdam to Marseille in 6.5hr.

The B.III long-range reconnaissance flying boat found no buyers, and neither did its civil version with a passenger cabin.

After the Ford Reliability Tour Fokker made the F.VIIA/3m prototype available to the Army Air Corps for testing from Wright Field. Pilots stood in long lines to be the first to fly it; the eight passenger seats were, of course, occupied by relatives. After this military goodwill tour, the aircraft was flown to Detroit to be inspected by Edsel Ford, who purchased it. He then made the aircraft available to Lt Commander Richard Byrd, who used it to become the first to fly an aircraft over the North Pole. The Fokker Atlantic Corporation of America was expanding rapidly. In 1926 Fokker already had eight dealers, each of whom had a Universal available.

Captain Hubert Wilkins bought one for use with an F.VIIB/3m on his Polar Expedition. Continental Motors purchased one as "executive aircraft" (probably the world's first business aircraft), and the Philadelphia Transit Company operated a scheduled service with F.VIIA/3ms.

Two new versions of the successful range of C.V scout aircraft appeared in 1926, with modernised wings. The D version was a fighter/tactical scout with a wing span of 12.5m, and the E version was a light bomber/strategic scout with a wing span of 15.3m. CVs with various engines were delivered to the Dutch Aviation Department, Naval Air Service and Royal Dutch East Indies Army, and to Bolivia, China, Denmark, Finland, Hungary, Italy, Japan, Norway, Sweden and Switzerland. The aircraft was manufactured under license in five countries.

Two Danish C.VE scouts carried out a long-distance flight to gain experience and show the flag. One was damaged in Burma, but the other flew on to Tokyo with Captain Botved and fitter Olsen aboard. They returned via Russia, completing an outstanding performance by a single-engined, open cockpit aircraft.

In 1926 the second stage was reached of KLM's future Dutch East Indies route. Grasé, together with van Os as co-pilot flew five passengers and mail non-stop from Rotterdam to Marseille in 6.5h to link with the steamer *Indrapoera* of the Rotterdam Lloyd, which was ready to depart.

That same year Fokker built yet another flying boat, the B.III long-range reconnaissance aircraft. However, it was not successful. Even after installing a cabin to adapt it for civil use, he was unable to find a buyer.

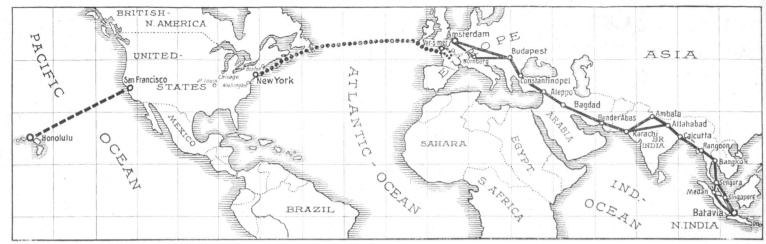

A route map showing three historic flights by Fokker aircraft. The dash-line on the left shows Maitland and Hegenberger's route, the dotted line shows Byrd's route, and the straight lines show the route of Van Lear Black.

Businessman Van Lear Black came to KLM in February 1927 to hire an aircraft and crew to take him to Cairo, where he wanted to surprise a friend with a sudden and unexpected visit. The flight was broken off at Belgrade, but heralded the start of a series of world-wide flights, first with chartered KLM aircraft and later with his own, though all were Fokker machines. From June 15th to July 23rd he made the first Amsterdam-Batavia round trip. This was also the first intercontinental charter flight in the world.

On the left: The departure of H-NADP, an F.VIIA. The following year he flew a three-engined F.VIIB/3m which bore the same registration. In 1928 he bought his own F.VIIB/3m, G-AADZ.

Drawings on opposite page. *Top: The F.VII H-NACC used for KLM's first flight to the Dutch East Indies in 1924.*

Centre: F.VIIA H-NACT, was the first commercial airliner in the world with an air-cooled radial engine.
Below: The F.VIIB/3m, the successful three-engined version of the F.VIIA.

Left: The extra fuel tank in the fuselage of the C-2 America could hold 3,000 litres. C-2 was the military designation of the American Fokker F.VIIB/3m. Byrd, accompanied by Noville, Acosta and Balchen, flew her from New York to Paris on June 29th, 1927. A dense fog over Paris forced Balchen to return to the coast, where he put the Fokker down in the sea a few metres from the beach (photograph below).

Below left: In order to get the overloaded aircraft off the ground, a take-off ramp was constructed on Fokker's advice. The take-off was made by Acosta. The weather en route was extremely bad, especially towards the end, when the route was obstructed by fog. For 19hrs they saw neither sea nor sky.

THIJS POSTMA

Above: An F.VIII of KLM, who bought seven. One of them, PH-OTO, was later converted to have two engines positioned in the wing leading edge.

Below left: One of the two F.VIIIs built by Manfred Weiss in Hungary completed as a bomber with two machine-gun posts. Below: A civil Hungarian F.VIII.

On June 28/29, 1927, Lieutenants Lester J. Maitland and Albert F. Hegenberger, flew a Fokker C-2 from San Francisco to Honolulu – the longest distance flown over water at that time. The 3,860km flight was approximately 800km further than from Newfoundland to Eire.. Left: Gradients were painted on the tailplane to aid navigation. Below left: A view of the C-2. Below, left to right: Fokker, Lt Maitland and Lt Hegenberger. Note Fokker's scruffy clothing.

The Fokker F.X was a bigger version of the 12-seater F.X airliner. It had seats for 14 passengers and was used on American routes. The US Army used one as the C-5 and one flew with the USMC as the RA-4.

The Super Universal was an enlarged Universal with an enclosed cockpit and improved undercarriage.

Pan American Airways flew F.XAs between Key West and Havana, Cuba, a route which included 100 miles over the sea.

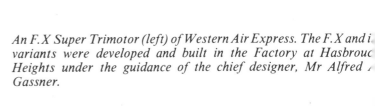

An F.X Super Trimotor (left) of Western Air Express. The F.X and its variants were developed and built in the Factory at Hasbrouck Heights under the guidance of the chief designer, Mr Alfred Gassner.

Below: A T-IV bomber/reconnaissance aircraft. From 1927 to 1941 12 T-IVs were in service with the Naval Air Service.

The F.VIII, a twin-engined airliner for KLM. Originally built as a 12-seater, it was later adapted to accommodate 15 passengers.

The cabin of the Postduif, *with extra fuel and oil tanks. A spare propeller is fastened to the right-hand side.*

The Postduif *and crew. From left to right, pilot G.M.H. Frijns, Captain G.A. Koppen and flight engineer S. Elleman. On October 1st, 1927, the Fokker F.VIIA/3m H-NAEA* Postduif *started for the first return mail flight to the Dutch East Indies. While Van der Hoop in H-NACC and Geysendorffer in H-NADP had to choose a route giving them ample opportunities to land in case of engine failure, Koppen, flying a three-engined aircraft, was able to select the shortest route over mountains and seas.*

Below: The route flown by the Postduif. *("Uitreis" = Outward-bound trip.)*

In 1927 Fokker's name made the headlines of the world's press when his aeroplanes made many historic flights. From June 15th to July 23rd, a Fokker F.VIIA made the first Amsterdam-Batavia return flight. This was also the world's first intercontinental charter flight, the aircraft having been chartered by the American millionaire Van Lear Black. Two months later, on October 1st, Lt Koppen of the Aviation Department, together with Frijns as second pilot and Elleman as flight mechanic, flew to the Dutch East Indies in record time in the F.VIIA/3m *Postduif*, carrying mail only.

Lieutenant Schott, flying an Aviation Department C.V, took part in the International Competition at Zürich, won the Alpine flight and so gained the Echard Trophy. The F.VIII, a new 15-seater, was built for KLM, and the T.IV, a large torpedo-bomber/scout on floats, was produced for the Naval Air Service.

In America Fokker was expanding again. At Brighton Mills, a few miles from Hasbrouck Heights, a second factory was brought into use, and a larger version of the successful Universal, the Super Universal, was built. In April the first F.X made its debut. Western Air was first to buy, with an order for three of these 12-seat airliners. Pan American, flying yet another F.X, the F.XA, with room for 14 passengers, operated between Key West and Cuba. The American Army and the Marines also obtained versions of the F.X.

US Air Corps pilots Maitland and Hegenberger flew a C-2 from San Francisco to Honolulu on June 28/29, the first flight over the Pacific from America to Hawaii. Also on June 29th, Richard Byrd flew in the C-2 *America* from New York to the city of Paris. However, a dense fog over Paris forced the pilot, Balchen to return to the coast, where he put the aircraft down exactly on a few landing flares which he had dropped previously. The *America* sank as far as its wing, and when the aircraft was brought ashore by the French Navy and fishermen from Ver-sur-Mer, it was immediately plundered by a crowd of souvenir hunters. Not a single thread of linen remained on the fuselage, cables were ripped out, and even the plywood wing covering was torn away by the panel.

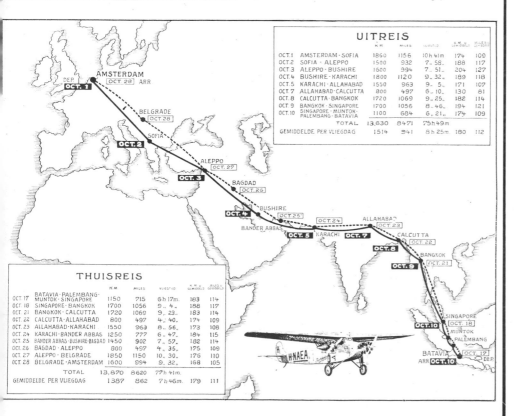

UITREIS

		K.M.	MILES	VLIEGTIJD	K.M. GEMIDDELD	MILES GEMIDDELD
OCT.1	AMSTERDAM-SOFIA	1860	1156	10 h 41 m	174	109
OCT.2	SOFIA-ALEPPO	1500	932	7 „ 58 „	188	117
OCT.3	ALEPPO-BUSHIRE	1600	994	7 „ 51 „	204	127
OCT.4	BUSHIRE-KARACHI	1800	1120	9 „ 32 „	189	118
OCT.5	KARACHI-ALLAHABAD	1550	963	9 „ 5 „	171	107
OCT.7	ALLAHABAD-CALCUTTA	800	497	6 „ 10 „	130	81
OCT.8	CALCUTTA-BANGKOK	1720	1069	9 „ 25 „	182	114
OCT.9	BANGKOK-SINGAPORE	1700	1056	8 „ 46 „	194	121
OCT.10	SINGAPORE-MUNTOK-PALEMBANG-BATAVIA	1100	684	6 „ 21 „	174	109
	TOTAL	13,630	8471	75 h 49 m		
	GEMIDDELDE PER VLIEGDAG	1514	941	8 h 25 m	180	112

THUISREIS

		K.M.	MILES	VLIEGTIJD	K.M. GEMIDDELD	MILES GEMIDDELD
OCT.17	BATAVIA-PALEMBANG-MUNTOK-SINGAPORE	1150	715	6 h 17 m	183	114
OCT.18	SINGAPORE-BANGKOK	1700	1056	9 „ 4 „	188	117
OCT.21	BANGKOK-CALCUTTA	1720	1069	9 „ 23 „	183	114
OCT.22	CALCUTTA-ALLAHABAD	800	497	4 „ 40 „	174	109
OCT.23	ALLAHABAD-KARACHI	1550	963	8 „ 56 „	173	108
OCT.24	KARACHI-BANDER ABBAS	1250	777	6 „ 47 „	184	115
OCT.25	BANDER ABBAS-BUSHIRE-BAGDAD	1450	902	7 „ 57 „	182	114
OCT.26	BAGDAD-ALEPPO	800	497	4 „ 35 „	175	109
OCT.27	ALEPPO-BELGRADE	1850	1150	10 „ 30 „	176	110
OCT.28	BELGRADE-AMSTERDAM	1600	994	9 „ 32 „	168	105
	TOTAL	13,870	8620	77 h 41 m		
	GEMIDDELDE PER VLIEGDAG	1387	862	7 h 46 m	179	111

The F.XI was a "feeder liner" and air taxi, and was similar to the American Universal in appearance. However, it was definitely not the same aircraft. The Universal was designed in America by Bob Noordwyn; the F.XI in Holland. The aircraft could carry four to six passengers and two pilots. Three aircraft of this type were built, two going to the Hungarian Company Malert (photo top), and the third to the Swiss Company Alpar (photo left). In 1954 a collision ended its flying career. This F.XI, fully restored, is now in Melbourne, Australia, where it is painted to represent the first Universal flown by Reginald Ansett. Confusion about its identity still reigns, apparently.

Below: The C.VIIW seaplane was built for reconnaissance and advanced training. Fokker built 30, all of which were delivered to the Naval Air Service.

The three-seater C.VIII reconnaissance/bomber was the response to a request from the Aviation Department to make a larger reconnaissance aircraft than ever before.

Below: The Royal Dutch East Indies Army took over two F.VIIB/3ms, equipped with Titan engines, from the Royal Dutch East Indies Airlines Company. They also used five F.VIIB/3ms with Lynx engines. The letters FTA stood for "Fokker Transport Ambulance".

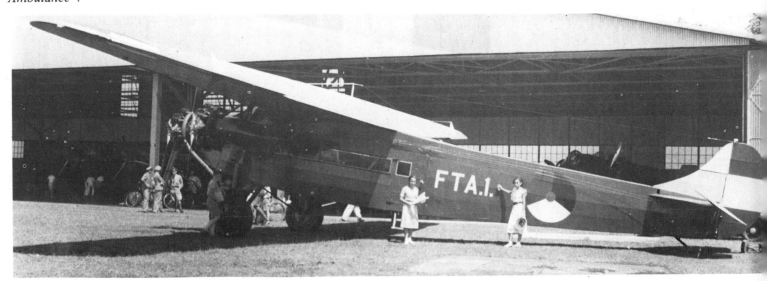

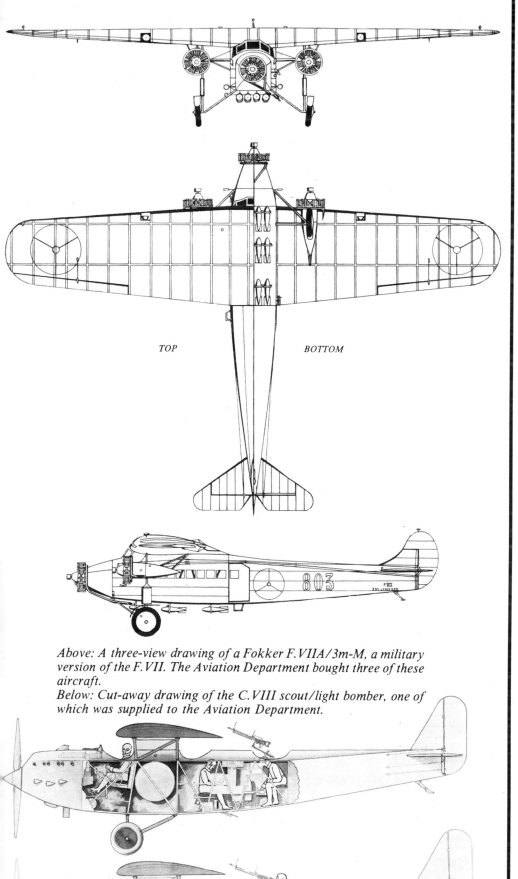

TOP   BOTTOM

Above: A three-view drawing of a Fokker F.VIIA/3m-M, a military version of the F.VII. The Aviation Department bought three of these aircraft.
Below: Cut-away drawing of the C.VIII scout/light bomber, one of which was supplied to the Aviation Department.

1928

In 1928 Fokker again received more than his share of the world-wide publicity. On June 17 and 18 Amelia Earhart, with Wilmer Stulz as pilot and Gordon as flight-engineer, became the first woman to fly across the Northern part of the Atlantic. The aircraft was an F.VIIB/3m fitted with floats – another "first".

Kingsford Smith in his *Southern Cross*, became the first pilot to bridge the Pacific from America to Australia, from May 31st to June 9th, and the Swede Lundborg used his Fokker C.V to save Nobile from the pack-ice on June 23rd.

Business couldn't have been better for Fokker. Licensing rights were sold to Italy, Japan and England. Even the French CIDNA Company purchased seven F.VI-IAs and three F.VIIB/3m aircraft, the first time that the French Government had permitted the purchase of foreign aircraft.

In August a third Fokker factory was opened in America, at Glendale. The American and Dutch Fokker factories put eleven new models and their variants on the market in 1928.

The XLB 2 was a bomber developed by the American Fokker factory and based on the F.VII/3m, the military designation of which was C-2. The XLB-2 had two Pratt & Whitney Hornet radial engines of 525 h.p. each. An observer/bomb-aimer, armed with a machine gun, was positioned in the nose.

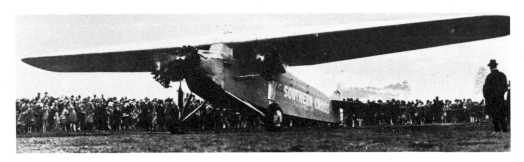

The Australian Captain Charles Kingsford Smith, with Ulm as second pilot, navigator Lyon and radio telegraphist Warner, covered the longest distance ever flown over water, from America to Australia, between May 31st and June 9th, 1928. This was the first time that the Pacific had been flown. Their aircraft, the Southern Cross, was an F.VI-IB/3m with Wright engines.

The B.IVA amphibian flying boat. The wheel axles were housed in stabilising floats which balanced the aircraft on water. During flight the wheels were retracted into recesses at the ends of the floats to reduce drag. Another designation for the B.IVA was F.XIA "Flying Yacht". A number of these aircraft were sold, to companies as well as to individuals. The picture below left shows Anthony Fokker in the door-way. Note the man with the trade-mark "Fokker" on his back, who "quite accidently" happened to sit on the wing, leaning against the engine with his back turned to the photographer.

Below: The original version of the B.IVA, the B.IV, also known as F.XI. A pure flying boat, only one was built. Twenty metal fuselages were constructed in Amsterdam, the B.IVA wings being made in America. The B.IVA was the first Fokker flying boat to achieve any success, only one example of each of its predecessors having been made.

Using this Fokker F.VII/3m, the Friendship, Amelia Earhart, together with pilot Wilmer Stulz and flight mechanic Lou Gordon, made the first flight of a float-equipped aircraft from America to England on June 17/18th, 1928. The photograph on the left shows the aircraft equipped with wheels. The Friendship was originally part of Byrd's first South Pole Expedition, but at the last moment he changed his mind and chose a Ford aircraft. Over the North Pole he had gained the impression that he was flying with a Fokker label round his neck. Amelia Earhart, who bought the aircraft, had not yet become famous, but was still quite a novice.

An F.VIIB/3m of Japan Air Transport, which operated regular services beginning in spring 1929.

Below: On June 23rd, 1928 the Swedish Lieutenant Einar Lundborg succeeded in rescuing the Italian General Nobile from the pack-ice where he and some of his crew were stranded. His airship had crashed on the ice on May 25th, bouncing off and leaving behind the gondola containing Nobile and part of his crew. The other six crewmembers went up again with the airship to their deaths. The picture shows Lundborg's C.V after a second landing, when the skis of his aircraft hooked under a tipping ice-floe.

A Super Universal of the Japan Air Transport Company, who imported ten of these aircraft in 1929. Later the type was built under license by the Japanese Nakajima Company, the first Japanese-built machine being delivered in March 1931. A total of 47 was built up to October 1936.

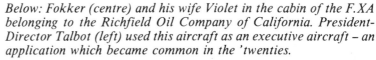

Below: Fokker (centre) and his wife Violet in the cabin of the F.XA belonging to the Richfield Oil Company of California. President-Director Talbot (left) used this aircraft as an executive aircraft – an application which became common in the 'twenties.

The three-engined F.XIV/3m, the passenger-carrying version of the F.XIV. This aircraft finished up in a playground at Soesterdal.

The F.XIV freighter in its original form. Owing to the financia depression the aircraft was not successful.

The C.IA was a modernised C.I with a radial engine. Although the flight characteristics were not improved, the Aviation Department converted 21.

The F.IX, a 20-passenger airliner, two of which went into service wit KLM. It was built under license in Czechoslovakia.

Right: The XO-27 was an American-designed reconnaissance aircraft with a crew of three. Two were built, one of which was converted to a bomber, the XB-8, in 1931. In 1931/32 the American Army ordered twelve O-27 bombers with larger wings, their engines being almost completely housed in the wing to reduce drag.

Below left: The Naval Air Service shed a Schellingwoude, near Amsterdam, wher many of Fokker's seaplanes were teste Although it was a naval establishment, som Fokker employees worked there.

Cross-sectional drawing of the C.VIII sea plane. The Dutch Naval Air Service pur chased nine C.VIIIWs, which had three-ma crews.

The C-14, top, was a US Army freighter aircraft. It was the military version of the American F.XIV, below. An ambulance version was designated C-15.

Above: The American F.XIV was a seven- to nine-passenger aircraft and had no similarity with the Dutch F.XIV, and was a parasol monoplane. The XIVA was a modified version with an enclosed cockpit in front of the wing.

Below: Fokker (with his hat in his arms) and his technical staff in America in 1929.

In this year Fokker aeroplanes again made many flights of international importance. The year commenced with a duration flight by the US Army C-2A *Question Mark*, which lasted 150hr and 40min. The American businessman Van Lear Black made a London to Cape Town return trip from February to April, and in June and July Kingsford-Smith flew from Australia to England in 13 days.

In August the Duchess of Bedford made a flight from England to India and back, in less than 8 days in a former KLM F.VIIA aircraft. On September 12th KLM opened the world's longest airline route, from Amsterdam to Batavia, using Fokker F.VIIB/3ms.

By the late 'twenties, the American Fokker Corporation had become the biggest aircraft producer in the world. The company had some 906 employees (plus 548 in Holland) and the orders kept coming in. In May, General Motors acquired 40 per cent of the shares. Fokker, who owned 20 per cent, was engaged as technical manager, but found it difficult to work with the management, which had come almost completely from the automobile industry. Professional market research, carried out by prominent people in General Motors, proved by means of impressive graphs that almost everyone would possess his own aircraft in the near future. This fact had, of course, escaped the simple Dutchman. Slowly but gradually, the Fokker factories in America slid downhill.

In October Fokker visited Holland in connection with the tenth anniversary of the founding of the Dutch factory. In 1929 his wife, Violet Fokker-Eastman, lost her life in an accident. Bertus Grasé, the phenomenal Fokker test-pilot who combined scientific education with an instinctive sense of flying, also died in the summer of that year. It was an almost insurmountable loss. The Naval Air Service and the Aviation Department loaned the company some pilots until Lieutenant Sandberg, an exceptional pilot, joined Fokker.

Top: A formation of D.XVIs of the Aviation Department. This fighter replaced the ten-year-old D.VII in 1929. At first the D.XVI was not impressive as a fighter. Its 460 h.p. Jaguar engine usually seized up after a few hours. This problem became so widespread that the aircraft were only permitted to fly in the vicinity of their own field, and long climbs were forbidden. Finally the "factory" (technical services) located at Soesterberg reduced away the pistons and solved the problem, though the D.XVI now used ten litres of oil per hour!
Of the 15 ordered by the Aviation Department, five crashed within a short space of time; the other ten flew without mishap. The D.XVI was very popular with pilots, in spite of its teething troubles.
Four Jupiter-engined D.XVIs were sold to Hungary, and one was built for Italy but later sold to China. Another was fitted with a Curtiss Conqueror engine for the Royal Dutch East Indies Army, but orders failed to materialise.

The sleeping cabin of the largest Fokker aircraft ever built; the F.XXXII. As a night-liner it could accommodate 16 passengers, but in normal configuration it seated 32. Hence the designation F.XXXII. Its four 525 h.p. Wasp engines were later replaced by 575 h.p. Hornets. The engines were suspended in tandem beneath the wing, and this led to cooling problems for the hindmost pusher units. The F.XXXII was designed for Universal Air Lines, which had ordered five, but after an accident with the prototype, they cancelled their order.

Above: Lt Sandberg, Bart., in front of the D.XVI with which he defended the Coupe Echard on behalf of the Aviation Department on July 31st, 1932, who had won the Cup in 1929. He had to pay his own expenses.
Below: Lt Wittert van Hoogland, Bart., lost his ailerons in a dive and crashed into the woods, losing his wings!

Above and below: Western Air Express tested two F.XXXIIs on their San Francisco-Los Angeles route, and ordered three more.

"AMERICA'S GREATEST AIR PASSENGER SYSTEM"... *Now Flies*

America's Largest Planes

ATTENTION AIRMEN!

Even you who count flying as your "bread-and-butter" business have a new experience awaiting—when you ride in America's largest craft and inspect the many new features. Your appreciated custom of choosing Western Air Express for personal transportation now leads you to a rare treat next trip.

WESTERN AIR EXPRESS, the pioneer, keeps the swift pace of leadership . . . assures continued dominance of the air lanes by introducing a fleet of Fokker F-32's to meet the demands of increasing traffic.

No larger ships, no liners more luxurious exist in America. The new Fokker F-32 represents the pinnacle of achievement in the entire industry.

Its adoption by Western Air Express is but another expression of the policy of constant progress to which "America's Greatest Air Passenger System is dedicated.

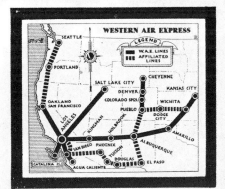

New York   **OFFICES**   Chicago
Graybar Bldg.   Kansas City   Palmer House

General Passenger Agent, Los Angeles

WESTERN AIR EXPRESS

...the Air Line that Airmen Choose for Personal Transportation

A Western Air Express advertisement in the April issue of Aero Digest *in 1930.*

Between January 1st and 7th, 1929, the Fokker F.VIIB/3m (U.
Army Air Corps C-2A) *Question Mark* set a world duration recor
of 150hr 40min, covering 17,000km at an average speed o
112km/hr. A total of 37 airborne contacts was made with a suppl
aircraft to transfer 19,000 litres of petrol, 950 litres of oil, 900kgs o
food and other stores. The crew received 19 complete hot meals, mor
than 200 litres of ice cream, telegrams, letters, a collapsible bathin,
tub, towels, woollen underwear, a rubber suit for Major Spaatz,
spare window for the cabin to replace one that was broken, and man
other items. The altitude during the flight varied from 900 to 1,20
metres.

Left: *The US Army Air Corps C-2A* Question Mark *during one of th
37 occasions when it was replenished in the air. Below left: A fligh
mechanic climbs out of the door on to a tubular frame, to go forwar
to make a necessary engine inspection and top up the oil.*

Below: Question Mark's *crew, from left to right: Maj Carl Spaatz
Capt Eaker, Lt Halverson, Lt Quesada and Sgt Hooe.*

Left: *The XA-7 was an all-metal attack aircraft. It appeared in 193C
and was a product of the General Aviation Corporation, as the former Fokker Factories were now named. The Army finally selectea
the Curtiss XA-8, which had been designed to the same specification.*

Below left: *The* Maryland Free State *of Van Lear Black. He flew
thousands of miles with the F.VII H-NADP of KLM, first in its
single-engined version and later as a trimotor. In 1928 Fokker buil,
him a new aircraft, G-AADZ, which was the property of an English
company founded by Van Lear Black.*

Below: *The F.VIIA* Spider, *owned by the Duchess of Bedford.*

In 1933 Fokker produced the F.XII, above, an airliner with three 420 h.p. Wasp engines and accommodation for 16 passengers. Eleven were built in Holland and two in Denmark.

Picture above and drawing below: The C.IX was a heavier version of the C.VE. Five were delivered to the Aviation Department and one to Switzerland.

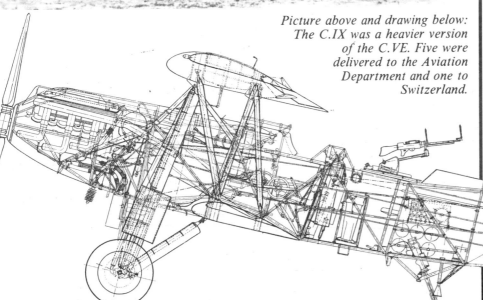

Fokker, now 40 years old, could still not complain about lack of publicity; the international headlines continued to report remarkable flights with Fokker aircraft.

Around the turn of the year the famous Swiss pilot Walter Mittelholzer, co-pilot Künzle and Baron Louis von Rothschild, together with some friends, carried out a charter flight to the Kilimanjaro area in an F.VIIB/3m. The Duchess of Bedford was also in the news again. In her single-engined Fokker F.VIIA, G-EBTS *Spider*, she made a return flight from London to Cape Town in 20 days in April 1930, beating the previous best time by more than two months. At first this elderly sportswoman flew as a passenger, but later on she piloted the aircraft herself. Van Lear Black made a flight from London to Tokyo in his Fokker F.VIIB/3m, but in August he disappeared without trace from his yacht near the Coast of New Jersey. He was 55 years old.

In June, Kingsford-Smith, in his world-famous *Southern Cross*, carried out the first completely successful East-West transatlantic flight. In America, the name Fokker Aircraft Corporation was changed to General Aviation Corporation.

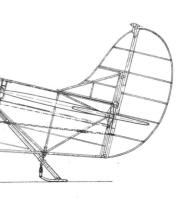

The Duchess of Bedford with her crew. On the left is Capt Barnard and on the right "Bob" Little. Apart from being a pilot, she was a skating champion, and could shoot and fish with the best.

Above: Kingsford-Smith's F.VIIB/3m Southern Cross *at Schiphol*

On June 24th, 1930, the Southern Cross *took off from the beach a*
Portmarnock, Ireland, to cross the Atlantic from East to West. Firs
pilot and owner was Charles Edward Kingsford-Smith. As a pilot ii
the Royal Flying Corps in 1917 he was badly wounded in a comba
with von Richthofen. He managed, however, to fly his aircraft bac
behind his own lines. After the First World War he worked succes
sively in British and American civil aviation. Great fame wa
accorded him after his flight across the Pacific, described on page 78
His second pilot on the Atlantic flight was Evert van Dijk, the naviga
tor was Jonathan Patrick Saul, and John Stanley Warburton Stan
nage was the radio operator.

Left: *The navigation compartment of the* Southern Cross. *The large*
extra fuel tank in the fuselage is well portrayed in this photograph

Below, rear row: *John Scholte, A.H.G. Fokker, Geyssendorffer.*
Front row: *Chamberlain, John Stannage, Patrick Saul, Charles*
Kingsford-Smith, Evert van Dijk, Bernt Balchen and Fitzmaurice.

Above: A PJ-2 of the US Coast Guard. This aircraft was converted by the Naval Aircraft Factory from a PJ-1, with pusher propellers, to the PJ-2 tractor.

Fokker was the winner of a competition instigated by the US Coast Guard for an FLB (Flying Life Boat) for patrol and rescue in the open sea. Because the American Fokker Factory was owned by the General Aviation Corp, at that time, the five flying boats ordered were designated GA-15, and the Coast Guard designation was PJ-1. They had a four-man crew and were equipped with two 420 h.p. Wasp engines driving pusher propellers. The first aircraft was converted by the Naval Aircraft Factory to PJ-2, with tractor propellers. The PJ flying boats were the last Fokker aircraft built in America until 1958. In 1935 General Aviation became North American Aviation, now Rockwell International.

Above: The PJ-1 flying boat, developed from the B.4A amphibious aircraft. All PJs were equipped with an undercarriage to enable them to beach under their own power (see photograph below).

In 1931 Fokker hit trouble in America. The wing of a TWA Fokker trimotor failed during a thunderstorm on March 31st, and the aircraft crashed. Among the seven victims was Knute Rockne, the coach of the famous Notre Dame football team, and the accident was treated as a national disaster. For a week it was front page news, and on May 4th the news came that all three-engined Fokker aircraft built in 1929 were to be grounded, as they were considered unsafe and had to be returned to the factory for inspection. Thirty-five aircraft, mainly belonging to Pan American, Western Air Express and American Airways, were taken out of service. Within two weeks the restriction was cancelled, as it was apparent that nothing was wrong with the aeroplanes, but the damage had been done.

Fokker aircraft, which had hitherto been considered the safest in the world, now had an undeserved reputation for weakness in America, and the operators replaced them by other types. TWA even burned a number of F.Xs. Relations between General Aviation and Fokker went from bad to worse, and on July 10th, 1931, a decisive meeting was held. In a battle of words Fokker, together with his lawyer Zachry, managed to ensure that his annual salary of $50,000 would be paid during the next five-year period, and also to maintain his right to use the name Fokker for business purposes. However, his right of entry into the factories was denied. General Motors prepared a press release, stating that the meeting had passed in harmony, and that Fokker would withdraw as technical director. When the directors left the building on Broadway after the meeting, they found that the newsboys were selling evening papers in which the result of the meeting was already described.

A telephone call to a friend by Fokker, made during the meeting, was the signal to various editors that his terms and conditions (about which they had already been informed) had been met.

General Aviation completed the current orders and the production of Fokker aircraft then came to a standstill until 1958, when the first American-built F.27 Friendship was delivered.

In Holland, Rheinhold Platz left the factory and was succeeded by F.H. Hentzen on April 1st. Also in 1931, Fokker published his autobiography *The Flying Dutchman*, which aroused a storm of reactions.

Above: A series of D.XVII fighters of the Aviation Department. The D.XVII was the last biplane to be built by Fokker, and the first design to be executed under the guidance of Mr Beeling. The prototype, with a Curtiss Conqueror engine (see drawing below), first flew in 1931, and was built to a specification issued by the Royal Dutch East Indies Army. It was delivered in 1932.

The authorities in Holland were sufficiently impressed with its performance to place an order for ten of the type, powered by 580 h.p. Rolls-Royce Kestrel engines. The D.XVIIs of the Aviation Department were in use until 1940, when they were still being used for war operations. Maximum speed was 356 km/hr at 4,000 metres, and the armament consisted of two machine guns.

Left: The cockpit of the D.XVII.

Below left: Lt Wittert van Hoogland, Bart, who, in 1935, obtained the Dutch altitude record in a D.XVII, reaching 10,180 metres. The actual height reached must have been about 11,000 metres, but during the record flight the pilot passed out because his oxygen mask became blocked at a temperature of −54° centigrade. He recovered at low altitude, the well-behaved D.XVII having spiralled down of its own accord.

Below: Cross-sectional drawing of the prototype D.XVII with the Curtiss Conqueror engine.

Bottom of page: A D.XVII with an experimentally-installed Lorraine-Dietrich engine.

The F.XX Zilvermeeuw, *constructed under the guidance of Ing Beeling.*

THIJS POSTMA

THIJS POSTMA

Carpenters in the woodworking section of the Fokker Factory, Papaverweg, Amsterdam. Note the youth of some workers. The little boy at top right, in cloth cap and tie for the photographer, looks 12 years old at the most.

Doping the linen-covered wings in the Werkspoor factory, Utrecht. During 1923 and 1924 approximately 800 wings were built here.

Below: Lt van Giessen of the Aviation Department in front of one of the two old D.VIIs which, during the Second International Polar Year, made daily meteorological flights near Reykjavik, Iceland.

Left: A KLM poster depicting a Fokker F.XXXVI. "Once legend, now reality".

At the beginning of the 'thirties Fokker aircraft were predominant in European airlines. Of the 17 European countries, the airlines of 13 operated with Fokker aircraft, and 17 factories had purchased the right to build under license. An important reason for this success was the method of construction used by Fokker. The fuselage and tailplane were made of welded steel tube of standard sizes, so that fuselage construction did not involve costly and ageing machinery. Repair and maintenance was also very simple, the linen-covered fuselage and other surfaces being easily accessible. If a fuselage required repairing, the damaged tube was cut away, and a new tube was inserted and welded. The wings were made of wood, always easily available and simply repaired. Carpenters and welders could, therefore, build Fokker aircraft without special tools. Moreover, the construction was very strong and resisted the weather extremely well. The Fokker aircraft which flew the route to the Dutch East Indies proved this beyond doubt. In spite of this, all was not going well for Fokker. He had lost his factories in the USA, and orders for his Dutch factory were diminishing. The number of employees reached an all-time low of 130; the economic crisis after the Wall Street crash of 1929 was having its effect.

Below: On October 19th, 1932, the Royal Netherlands Aeronautical Society awarded its Gold Medal to Anthony Fokker for promoting world aviation.

The F.XX Zilvermeeuw *was the first Fokker commercial aircraft with a retractable undercarriage. Apart from the engine attachment it was a well-streamlined aircraft, but the age of all-metal airliners had arrived, and Fokker was left behind. The aircraft carried 12 passengers at a cruising speed of 270 km/hr.*

Bottom of page: The F.XX under construction in the Amsterdam-North factory.

Below: Fokker and Ing Beeling, who was in charge of the project.

Below: The F.XX cockpit with its dual controls.

Below: The 12-passenger cabin of the F.XX.

Plesman (left) and Fokker (right), two great men of Dutch Aviation. It was the quality of its Fokker aircraft that made KLM great. Fokker was already famous when KLM was founded, but in the world of commercial aviation KLM enhanced Fokker's reputation. Plesman and Fokker did not always agree. For instance, in 1920, Plesman suggested that Fokker take back two F.IIs from KLM for the same price paid when they were new. Although Plesman argued that the F.IIIs they were buying would be beneficial to Fokker's name, Fokker would not agree.

Drawing below: The Lockheed Electra. Fokker acquired the licensing and sales rights for Europe and colonies from Lockheed, but in 1936 this contract was cancelled.

Photograph below: The Fokker factory's DC-2 demonstration aircraft. Fokker had the licensing and sales rights for Europe (except Russia), but although he paid $100,000 for them, the DC-2 was never produced by his company.

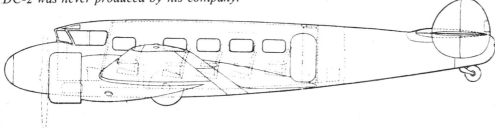

On July 1st, 1933, the first all-metal low-wing passenger aircraft with retractable undercarriage made its maiden flight. The Douglas DC-1 was to lead the DC-2, an aircraft of great importance to civil aviation. It was to signify the end of the reign of Fokker aircraft, with their welded steel tubing, wood and linen construction. On June 6th, 1932, KLM director Albert Plesman had discussed with Anthony Fokker the design of an entirely new, four-engined aircraft for the East Indies route, and had mentioned the possibility of an order for six aircraft in a letter following this discussion. The appearance of the DC-1 ended this interest abruptly. The modern, stream-lined DC-2, with its retractable landing gear, flaps and variable pitch propellers was, naturally, of greater appeal to Plesman.

On October 27th, 1933, Fokker cabled Douglas in America to acquire the licensing and sales rights for Europe, and (according to Fokker) paid at once. On November 8th, Plesman also cabled to Douglas. The aviation historian Henri Hegener wrote in his book *Fokker, the man and the aircraft*: "Two weeks later, on November 23rd, before he had received a reply to his cable and the letter which had followed the cable, Fokker gave him the surprise of his life. Dropping into Plesman's office, he announced with a suppressed smile that he had become a Douglas agent, and also had an option for manufacturing the aircraft in Holland." Fokker had beaten Plesman to it. Ing Wijdooge of KLM, who himself had been involved in the matter, counters by saying that Plesman repeatedly encouraged Fokker to acquire the licensing rights for the DC-2.

Whatever the case, Fokker signed the contract in the USA on January 15th, 1934. The F.XX, F.XXXVI and F.XXII had caused him substantial losses, but the sale of the DC-2 and the DC-3 put some money back in the till.

Fokker sold 39 DC-2s altogether, and 46 DC-3s. This was mainly due to the work of his super-salesman, Mr Seekatz. In addition, a Fokker F.XVIII, the *Pelikaan* made a fast Christmas mail flight to Batavia and put the name Fokker in the headlines yet again.

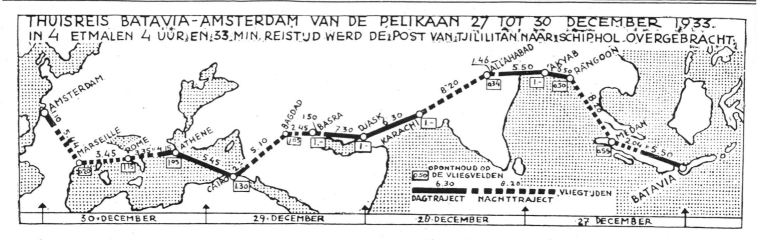

THUISREIS BATAVIA-AMSTERDAM VAN DE PELIKAAN 27 TOT 30 DECEMBER 1933.
IN 4 ETMALEN 4 UUR EN 33 MIN. REISTIJD WERD DE POST VAN TJILILITAN NAAR SCHIPHOL OVERGEBRACHT.

Above: Cutting from the newspaper De Telegraaf *January 2nd, 1934.*

Left: The crew of the Pelikaan, *from left to right, Smirnoff, (Captain), Soer, (co-pilot), Grosfeld and Van Beukering. Centre: Products of the souvenir industry, which did not want to miss the opportunity.*

Below: The Pelikaan *after touch-down at Schiphol Airfield. Some 20,000 people had gathered to welcome the crew. Those unable to come to Schiphol were glued to their wireless sets.*

106DE JAARGANG No. 34803

Nieuwe Amsterdamsche Courant

ALGEMEEN HANDELSBLAD

Dit nummer bestaat uit zes bladen   Directeur: A. HELDRING

Zondag 31 December 1933   Hoofdredacteur: D. J. von BALLUSECK

THE "PELIKAAN" LANDED ON SCHIPHOL AT 10.14 p.m.

Fog made landing difficult, forcing crew to circle for 30 minutes over the field before landing.

THE WHOLE CREW KNIGHTED WITH THE ORDER OF ORANJENASSAU

The *Pelikaan* landed at Schiphol yesterday evening at 10.14, having made her return flight within the record time made flying from Amsterdam to Batavia. The aircraft was over the field at 9.40 p.m., but could not land owing to the dense fog. For half an hour they tried repeatedly to find the field. The reception by thousands of people was impressive. Minister Kalff informed the crew that H.M. The Queen had appointed each crew member Knight of the Order of Oranje-Nassau. Burgomaster De Vlugt of Amsterdam handed the aviators the Silver Medal of the town.

A MOST IMPRESSIVE FINISH

The *Pelikaan* is back in its nest.

It has been accomplished, and with a sigh of relief Holland saw the fast bird land at its home at Schiphol. Immediately following the event, proud enthusiasm ignited to become a fanfare-like welcome to the "knights of the air" *par excellence*. Knights indeed – now that the government has awarded them with the Knight's Cross of the Order of Oranje-Nassau. A well-earned appreciation for the know-how and persistence, the bravery and the energy which they displayed, and also for this sporting "stunt" in a wider sense, as it may have far-reaching results for the airlink with the Dutch East Indies.

However, it is impossible to dwell upon this subject at present. The crew's report will be the basis for further studies, new trials and continued improvement of this excellent undertaking by KLM. At the moment it will have to be sufficient that we are a profoundly grateful nation, and offer our thanks to all concerned for this perfect and cheerful ending to the year. To the crew of the *Pelikaan* and to KLM who jointly made this happy outcome possible, go our gratitude and our homage.

The Christmas flight of the Pelikaan

Financed by the "Stoomvaart Maatschappij Nederland" and the "Rotterdamse Lloyd", at the initiation of Lieutenant D. Asjes, the Pander factory built a fast, specialised mailplane to compete with KLM. KLM therefore decided to prove that their normal scheduled service is just as fast and could be cheaper. For this purpose the new, fast F.XX "Zilvermeeuw" was chosen to take a large quantity of Christmas mail to Java. On the morning of the departure, the centre engine proved defective, so Plesman had the mail transferred to an F.XVIII, PH-AIP *Pelikaan*. Captain Ivan Smirnoff and his crew then saved the honour of the KLM by flying to Java and back in record time, the return to Schiphol being more spectacular than the rest of the journey. Schiphol was covered by a dense fog, and for forty minutes the *Pelikaan* circled overhead, while 20,000 spectators held their breath. All over Holland people were glued to their wireless sets. Suddenly the *Pelikaan* loomed out of the fog and came to a halt before an ecstatic public.

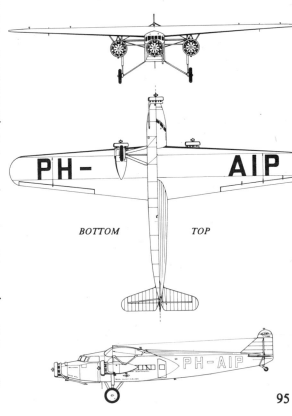

PH- AIP

BOTTOM   TOP

PH-AIP

Cuttings from the Algemeen Handelsblad *of Sunday, December 31st, 1933.*

Left: A cartoon out of a Fokker-Bulletin *of 1933. The caption read: Father Time: "Well, I'm damned, that one just ignores me! I shall have to get myself some Fokker wings to keep up with it."*

Right: A three-view drawing of the F.XVIII Pelikaan.

Cross-sectional drawing of the Fokker C.X.

Above: The C.X demonstration aircraft.

Below: A series of C.X scouts for the Aviation Department. After 14 C.Xs had been ordered for the Royal Dutch East Indies Army, the Aviation Department followed it with an order for 20 aircraft.

Above: Mr G. Sandberg, an outstanding demonstration pilot. He demonstrated Fokker aircraft in Rumania and China. Then, as a member of the Board of the Fokker Factory, he demonstrated the C.X in Ankara for the Turkish Government in 1935. During a vertical dive the wings broke off and Sandberg had no chance to use his parachute.

Photograph below left: This bomber-version of the Fokker F.IX was manufactured in Czechoslovakia, the example shown having been impressed by the Germans.

Drawing below left: The projected successor to the D.XVII was the D.XIX, but it was not built.

A formation of F.IX bombers in pre-war days.

Fokker with Lindbergh in the cockpit of the F.XXXVI under construction during the latter's visit to the factory. Note the staggered position of the seats.

Below: A Douglas DC-2 and Fokker F.XXXVI of KLM. The DC-2 marked the end of plans for series-production of the F.XXXVI.

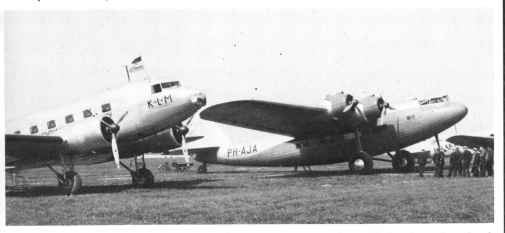

A cut-away drawing of the F.XXXVI, in the 16-passenger version with sleeping cabins for the East Indies route. The F.XXXVI was, however, only used on the European routes in the 32-passenger version.

The still-worsening situation of the Dutch Aircraft industry meant that Fokker could only survive by cutting into his reserves. These were not unlimited, and in May Fokker (and also KLM) turned to the Government for aid. A commission, chaired by Mr van Doorninck, was appointed to investigate and report the situation, and recommended the amalgamation of the Fokker, Koolhoven, Aviolanda and Pander factories. The role to be fulfilled by Fokker was not clear. However, the amalgamation did not come off. In 1940 the Koolhoven factory was bombed out of existence, and was never resurrected. Pander succumbed, after which the Royal Company De Schelde took over Pander's designer and a number of his staff.

Aviolanda, De Schelde and Fokker were eventually to unite, but not until long after World War Two, after yet another unsuccessful attempt. On June 22nd Fokker's test pilot Emil Meinecke made the maiden flight of the F.XXXVI, a comfortable giant destined for KLM's East Indies route. However, the advent of the DC-1 and its successors frustrated that plan. Another new Fokker type, the C.X, appeared. It was a scout which had been designed to the order of the Royal Dutch East Indies Army.

Chief designer Hentzen left the Fokker factory in March, and was succeeded by the former technical manager of Lufthansa, Dr Erich Schatzki, for whom it had become quite impossible to work in Germany after 1933. In December yet another historic flight was made with a Fokker F.XVIII when KLM's *Snip* flew from Schiphol to Curaçao in the Dutch Antilles, thereby forging the first air link between Holland and the Dutch Antilles.

THE FLIGHT TO THE DUTCH WEST INDIES

The Snip *in flight*

"SNIP" ARRIVED IN CURAÇAO

At 17.50 (Antillian Time) the aircraft landed at La Guaira and departed again exactly 30min later, landing at Willemstad (Curaçao) at 19.40.

On the night of December 14th/15th, 1934, Captain Hondong, co-pilot/navigator Van Balkom, telegrapher Van der Molen and flight-engineer Stolk, set off on the first Dutch transatlantic flight. Their KLM aircraft, the F.XVIII *Snip* was to be the first to cover the route from Holland to the Dutch West Indies by air.

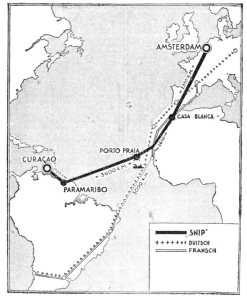

The route flown by the Snip.

THE GOAL IS REACHED

At 10.41 yesterday morning the *Snip* took off from Zanderij airfield near Paramaribo, and landed at La Guaira in Venezuela, after a fortuitous flight, at 17.50. After 30min rest, some fuel was taken aboard, the aircraft took off again to land on the island of Curaçao at exactly 19.40 (Amsterdam Time).

The flight to the West Indies has been accomplished. This is the proper place for a quiet salute, a word of appreciation for the pioneer work that has been carried out.

The West Indies have now been brought closer to the Motherland, as were the East Indies by the pioneering flight by Van der Hoop *et al* in 1924.

Out there – in the West – they will be happy, and justifiably so. Not because this flight foreshadows a regular schedule, but because it is apparently the firm intention of the Netherlands Aviation Company to include the West Indies in her airline-network.

The *Snip* has closed the gap. The Fokker F.XVIII will stay in the West as the first of a number of aircraft which are to be used for operating routes in the West Indies in the near future.

The flight from Amsterdam to Curaçao is, therefore, only to be considered as an incidental flight, with the establishment of an airline network in the West as its background, and publicity for commercial aviation as its immediate aim.

The pioneering of Jan Hondong, Van Balkom, Van der Molen and Stolk has, happily, been crowned with success.

The Goal has been reached!
We are grateful for that.
Precisely at this moment!

___

En route particulars

The smooth journey has obviously not been marred by any incidents. The messages sent by Van der Molen were apparently nothing more than position reports. This was hardly surprising, because the weather was very good all the time, the engines ran smoothly, and they had so much tailwind that an average speed of more than 200 km/hr could be achieved.

The *Snip* telegrapher had regular contact with various radio stations; mostly with Curaçao, Paramaribo and Venezuela. That so few messages were received is probably due to the fact that there was nothing remarkable to be reported during this "routine" flight.

At 17.50 (A.T.)

The West Indies aircraft has landed neatly on the airfield of La Guaira, where the Venezuelan authorities awaited Hondong and his crew.

The last leg

Exactly 30min later came the take off for the last 280 kilometres which separates La Guaira from Curaçao, a distance flown at a speed of more than 200 km/hr. Then the glad tidings arrived that the *Snip* had touched down on the airfield near Willemstad at 19.40 (A.T.), approximately a quarter to four local time.

The West Indies flight, Amsterdam-Curaçao, had a happy ending!

Below left: During the Second World War another F.XVIII, the Oriol *was converted to fight submarines. They exercised with flour bags.*

Below right: A hole was cut into the fuselage to house a machine gun.

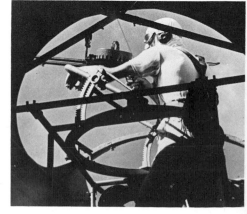

After ten years as a director Stephan left the Fokker factories, to be succeeded by van Tijen.

Below: The open cockpit Pander EG.100 sports aircraft used by van Tijen to fly to the Dutch East Indies in 1930.

In December 1933 the prototype of the DC-3, the great successor to the DC-2, flew for the first time. The Fokker F.27 was to succeed it many years later. Below, a photograph of a DC-3 for the Czechoslovakian company CLS being towed through the narrow streets of Cherbourg at night, after arriving by ship. Once on the airfield, a Fokker crew assembled and flight-tested the aircraft.

On January 25th the English aircraft company Airspeed came to an agreement with Fokker for the manufacture of DC-2s and various Fokker aircraft. Fokker was to act as technical advisor. However, owing to the threat of war, Airspeed received such large orders for the manufacture of aircraft that this came to naught. The agreement actually meant that Fokker gained financially from each aircraft sold, regardless of its type. Doing business still came naturally to Fokker. In November Bruno Stephan left the Fokker factory to start work as technical advisor for the Turkish Ministry of Defence. He had run the factory for ten years.

Fokker was always roaming about the world, sometimes in America, then in Switzerland, or in Holland if he was not travelling somewhere else. The day-to-day running of the factory was not his prime concern. Stephan was succeeded by van Tijen, who had been export manager with the Van Houten chocolate factory. Van Tijen had learned to fly in 1929 and, as a gliding pioneer, had met Fokker. He also took part in a balloon race. As a temporary crewmember, van Tijen had crossed the Atlantic aboard the airship *Graf Zeppelin*, and in 1930 he undertook a solo flight in an open sports aircraft from Schiphol to Java. Management and aviation were no strangers to him. Upon his arrival the financial situation of Fokker had improved slightly – at least, it was better than it had looked for the previous few years. The reason for this improvement was not a happy one. Slowly, even the most optimistic of the politicians realised that war was virtually unavoidable. Military orders were received in increasing numbers and for larger quantities. The naval scout seaplane C.XIW appeared, an improved version of the T.IV was delivered, and four new F.XXIIs came off the assembly line. A three-engined flying boat for the Navy, the B.V did not proceed beyond the design stage.

Above: The F.XXII Kwikstaart *in the foreground, with the F.XXXVI* Arend *behind. The F.XXII was a smaller version of the F.XXXVI, carrying 22 passengers – hence the designation. Three were built for KLM and one for the Swedish Company ABA.*

The C.XIW, below, was a scout seaplane for the Naval Air Service, designed to be catapulted from a warship. Fifteen were built.

Above: The F.XXII Kwikstaart for KLM during the final stages of completion.

Below: The same aircraft airborne.

Right: The announcement of the agreement between Airspeed and Fokker. See right-hand column, page 99.

Below right: In 1935 the T.IVA, an updated version of the T.IV was produced. However, it was an old aircraft, regardless of its new engines and enclosed cockpit and gun turrets. The original T.IV is shown on page 74.

Below: Turning over the 33-metre wing of the F.XXXVI in the "covering" department.

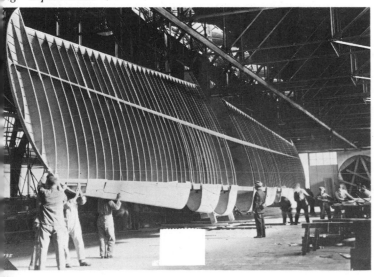

AIRSPEED
(1934) LIMITED

IMPORTANT AGREEMENT WITH *Fokker*

WE announce an important agreement, which was made on 25th January, 1935, between Mr. ANTHONY FOKKER, on behalf of N.V. NEDERLANDSCHE VLIEGTUIGENFABRIEK, and our Company.

By this Agreement, we have acquired the licence to manufacture in the United Kingdom, Channel Islands, Isle of Man, and the Irish Free State, fifteen of the Fokker types of aircraft. This Agreement covers the sale of these types within the United Kingdom, Isle of Man, Irish Free State, Channel Islands, India, British Empire and Dominions, British Colonies, Dependencies, Protectorates and Mandated Territories.

A further important part of the Agreement is for the manufacture and sale of the Douglas D.C.2 within the United Kingdom, Irish Free State, Channel Islands and Isle of Man. The Douglas D.C.2 is the most advanced, high-speed, passenger aircraft at present manufactured in America. It was one of these machines which, with a full complement of passengers, gained second place in the recent London/Melbourne Air Race. This machine was, at the same time, winner of the handicap section of the Race.

In addition to the important manufacturing rights which we have acquired, Mr. Fokker has agreed to act as our Technical and Aeronautical Adviser, in order to maintain the closest co-operation between our two interests.

The result of this arrangement will mean we are in a position to build in our factory aircraft to meet the most exacting requirements of the British Empire, including civil as well as military designs.

With this expansion, it will be possible to build the largest land and seaplanes for use on the British Empire Air Routes.

We trust that the linking of these interests will further the advancement of aviation in both countries.

AIRSPEED (1934) LIMITED.

Above and below: The prototype D.XXI.

Below: Dr Schatzki (left) and Meinecke in front of the D.XXI prototype.

On February 27th, 1936, the prototype of Fokker's first low-wing fighter to be produced in series, the D.XXI, took off from Welschap airfield near Eindhoven. It was designed to the order of the Royal Dutch East Indies Army. Dr Schatzki, who was in charge of the project, was aware that actually modern fighter aircraft of the period were designed as all-metal, low-wing aircraft with retractable undercarriages. However, Fokker could not afford the luxury of switching the factory over to the new methods. The D.XXI was, therefore, constructed according to the old Fokker recipe: fuselage and tailplane of welded steel tubing covered with linen and a wooden wing. The East Indies Army had requested a fixed undercarriage.

Ten days before the first flight of the D.XXI, Colijn, Minister for Colonial Affairs, announced that no fighters would be purchased for the Dutch East Indies, and that instead bombers were to be bought in America.

The Defence Minister asked the opinion of Col Best, Commander of the Aviation Department, with a view to a possible order for Holland. Col Best thought the D.XXI too slow, and did not like the fixed undercarriage. The construction of a prototype with a retractable undercarriage was too expensive, as it would have amounted to the enormous sum of almost DFL. 100,000 (the price of an expensive series-produced car today). After an intensive testing programme, however, 36 D.XXIs were ordered for the Aviation Department. Finland too and Denmark also ordered the D.XXI, and manufacture under license commenced in republican Spain.

Fokker amidst his employees on the occasion of his 25th anniversary as a pilot. The T.IVA's registration was T.13.

Above: The prototype D.XXI in the air. Production aircraft had a 760 h.p. Mercury engine and four machine guns for armament. The maximum speed was 460 km/hr.

Below: A replica of the Spin with two F.XXIIs. The Spin was demonstrated by Meinecke at the Jubilee flying display.

Below: A visit by Prince Bernhard to the Fokker factory in 1936. Next to the Prince is co-director van Tijen, and behind, from left to right, Vattier Crane (President of the Board), Vos Janszen and an unknown person.

The first Fokker monoplane fighter, which was to be series-produced in Holland, made its maiden flight this year. It was the D.XXI, manufactured under the supervision of Hentzen's successor, Schatzki. Fokker had still not changed to all-metal construction, and the D.XXI again employed the old, mixed construction methods. Also of a composite construction was the new fighter-bomber which Fokker was building in secret, the G.I, which was the sensation of the year at the Paris Air Show in 1936. More than four months later, on March 16th, 1937, the G.I made its maiden flight, and in December the Aviation Department ordered 36 G.IAs. This was a larger version with the then formidable armament of eight machine guns in the nose, and one in the rear of the fuselage nacelle.

Spain ordered a batch of the smaller G.IB, but these were not delivered, and the Dutch Government took over the aircraft at the end of 1939. In Holland they were known as "Finnish G.Is", but Finland had never ordered them.

In 1936 Fokker celebrated the 25th anniversary of the award of his pilot's licence. Everyone who had worked at the factory at least ten years received 100 guilders, and 10 guilders more for every additional year. A flying display was organised which included an F.II, a D.VII and a Spin, which was flown by test-pilot Meinecke. On the occasion of his jubilee Fokker put up some money to start the so-called "Fokker-Foundation", to provide financial support for less wealthy aspiring pilots, give tuition gratuities to people who wanted a place in aviation, and to further causes beneficial to Dutch aviation.

In July Plesman organised a meeting with Government officials and representatives from Fokker, Koolhoven and De Schelde, to discuss plans for a transatlantic aircraft. They progressed no further than talking, and three years later Plesman stated that he did not intend to purchase a "paper" aircraft.

Above: A Fokker advertisement of 1936. (Foreign press reviews)

Below: The prototype G.I with two 750 h.p. Hispano-Suiza engines.

Above: The prototype G.I at the Paris Air Show in 1936. The aircraft created a sensation with its twin booms and its armament of two cannon and two machine guns in the nose, plus another machine gun in the rear of the fuselage. In the photograph the nose-cone is missing. Sabotage caused the aircraft to drop from its hoist in Paris after the cables had been "treated" with sulphuric acid. A Fokker sheet-metal worker repaired the nose-cone in one afternoon!

TOMORROW'S FIGHTING 'PLANE

The *Figaro* acclaims Fokker's latest creation, the Fokker G.I.

AIRCRAFT WITH THREE APPLICATIONS

Under the heading: "Tomorrow's Fighting Plane", the Paris newspaper *Figaro* devotes an extensive article to the latest creation of the famous Dutch aircraft constructor, Anthony Fokker, the Fokker G.I, a twin-engined, two-seat aircraft which is exhibited at the 15th "Paris Salon d'Aviation", in the Grand Palace, Paris, and which has been named "Le Faucheur" (The Reaper). This name, writes André Reichel in *Figaro*, adequately describes the machine's role as a fighter/reconnaissance and light bomber-aircraft.

Since the Great War Fokker has produced aircraft of all types. His three-engined transport aircraft have served for long periods on the international airlines; not only in Europe, but even more so in America. In the sphere of commercial aviation Fokker has been able to obtain the licensing rights for building Douglas aircraft, and we believe that he acted wisely.

He has now put his efforts into the production of an ultra-modern prototype, destined for aerial combat, and our flying officers have shown more than the usual interest in this machine.

Being up to date is the major requirement for a war-time aircraft, and Fokker has not only taken into account every requirement which may concern aerial fighting, but has also incorporated those items which may be necessary in the future.

In general, one proceeds like this when constructing a fighting aircraft: first one builds an aircraft, and then one puts in the armament. Fokker, however, did it the other way round. He first thought about the armament, and then he built the aircraft around it, so to speak.

The problem which faced him was whether or not it would be possible to design an aircraft which could put an end to the activity of the heavy bombers as efficiently as possible. He had to design a fighter aircraft which also was a reconnaissance and light bombing aeroplane: fast and with a large radius of action. The Fokker G.I has all the advantages of a single-seat fighter, but possesses advantages which other existing aircraft do not have.

The armament of the G.I consists of two 23mm cannon and two fixed 7.9mm machine guns, installed in the nose of the aircraft, and a rotatable 7.9mm machine gun in the tail, fitted in a kind of turret. The aircraft can also carry a 400kg bomb-load.

Its maximum speed is 470 km/hr and the radius of action is approximately 1,400km. There is a two-man crew, so that the aircraft has excellent strategic reconnaissance potential.

The Fokker G.I's superiority is mainly founded on its enormous armament. To our knowledge no other fighter features such an arsenal.

The 23mm Madsen-cannon installed in the aircraft have several advantages over those of 20mm. Several armament authorities have doubted the effectiveness of a 20mm projectile and have expressed doubt as to whether a few shots would be sufficient to put an enemy aircraft out of action. The four fixed guns are operated by the pilot, who only has to pull a lever to operate them pneumatically and hydraulically.

The great speed and formidable climbing power of the aircraft renders it extremely suitable for attacking bombers.

As a reconnaissance aircraft it has a range of 1,600km, whilst as a bomber a load of 400kg can be carried, as stated before.

The "Fokker G.I" – states André Reichel in the conclusion of his article, which is highly complimentary, incorporates all the latest technical innovations.

Below: Test-pilot Meinecke demonstrates the G.I for the first time over the factory. All the employees went outside to watch this: at such a moment each man was as proud as if he had built the aircraft on his own.

Above: An article from the Nieuwe Rotterdamsche Courant *of November 20th, 1936.*

Below: The prototype G.I, with 825 h.p. Twin Wasp Junior engines. The Aviation Department objected to the Hispano-Suiza engine because their other aircraft had been equipped with the Bristol Mercury. Moreover, the Hispano 80-02 was new and untried.

Above: The prototype XIVW. This two-seater floatplane was designed for the Naval Air Service as a successor to the C.VIIW, and 24 were delivered before the outbreak of World War Two. During the mobilisation period (September 1939 – May 1940) the C.XIVs patrolled the coast and carried out reconnaissance flights.

Above: The prototype of the S.IX for the Aviation Department, who ordered 40. The first batch of 20 was delivered but for one, and a number escaped to France in May 1940.

Below: The prototype T.V 'cruiser' bomber. The Aviation Department ordered 16.

Under the ever-increasing threat of war, more and more military prototypes appeared. There was a shortage of pilots and, therefore, a demand for pupils and training aircraft. Additionally, the 15-year-old S.III of the Naval Air Service and the S.IV were overdue for replacement.

The C.XIVW trainer was ordered for the Naval Air Service, and also the S.IX, of which 15 were ordered. A year later the Aviation Department ordered 20, but with a different engine.

The G.I was modified, and an order for 36 followed. The prototype of the T.V 'cruiser' made its first flight. This aircraft was designed to cruise around in front of any area in need of protection, and to be fast and heavily armed, and able to carry sufficient fuel to cruise for long periods. The Aviation Department ordered 16, but by the time these aircraft were put into service, the whole conception was outdated. The secondary role of the T.V, that of bomber, now became its primary duty, but because only a few T.Vs had the proper bomb racks this task could not be properly executed.

Civil projects included an F.XXXVI with retractable undercarriage, the F.XXXVII and the four-engined double-decker F.LVI commercial aircraft. Neither of the last two was built.

A radical modernisation of constructional techniques could be postponed no longer, but Fokker was unable to finance such a programme himself. In May 1937, therefore, he went to the stockmarket. Up to then the factory had been a private company.

Right: A D.XXI patrol during the mobilisation period. The orange triangles on fuselage and wing and the orange rudder with black edges were the Dutch insignia after September 13th, 1939. On that date, a Dutch T.VIIIW, R.5, was shot down "in error" by a German aircraft. The Germans claimed that they had mistaken the original Dutch identification markings for British roundels, and the new insignia were introduced by Royal decree.

THIJS POSTMA

Opposite, top: A drawing of the Fokker C.V "631" during an unprotected reconnaissance of Valkenburg airfield on May 10th, 1940, between 10.00 and 10.30hr. In the background are the three Messerschmitts, that attacked the C.V and hit her, but were unable to prevent her escape. The pilot on this flight of "631" was Sgt van Schaik, and the observer was Capt van Mercelis Hartsinck. A few hours earlier this almost 15-year-old C.V had, with four others, bombed Valkenburg airfield. Two hours later, again without cover, it successfully bombed Ypenburg airfield. One hour after this bombing-run, the "631" again reconnoitred Valkenburg. On May 12th a reconnaissance in the vicinity of Arnhem was made with fighter protection. On May 14th "631" made its last operational flight to reconnoitre near Utrecht. Near Doorn the aircraft received multiple hits, but in spite of this it returned to its base.

On February 1st, 1931, Ing Marius Beeling, succeeded Dr Schatzki as chief designer. Beeling had come to Fokker as early as March 1923, as assistant to Rethel. In August 1929 he succeeded Ing Roosenschoon, as head of the scientific department. He played an important part in the development of the F.VII, F.XII and F.XVIII, and the F.XX and the F.XXXVI were mainly his creations, as were the D.XVII, G.I and T.IX. Ing Beeling succeeded in keeping the majority of his staff together during the occupation so that, after the Second World War, they could start up again with minimum effort.

After becoming sub-director and director of the Fokker Factory, he became professor of aircraft construction at the Technical College, Delft, and adviser to Avio-Diepen.

From 1956 to 1962 Beeling represented Fokker at Fairchild's. The conversations

which the author had with this amiable expert in the sphere of aircraft-manufacturing proved enormously helpful in the composing of this book.

Right: The Fokker T.V "856" pre-war.

Opposite, below: On May 13th, 1940, T.V number 856, accompanied by two G.Is, bombed the bridge near Moerdijk. During the first run a 300kg bomb detonated 50m from the bridge, and on the second run a bomb landed beside a bridge pillar but failed to explode. Immediately following the attack the aircraft dived to low altitude to return. North of Dordrecht, however, they were attacked by a group of Messerschmitt Bf109s. The GIs climbed to cover "856", but the pursuers split into three groups, each of which attacked one of the Dutch aircraft. In spite of the defence put up by its gunner, "856" was riddled with 20mm shells and crashed near Ridderkerk, killing the crew. According to the official history compiled by Col F.J. Molenaar (retd), and from which the above has been taken, "315" crashed in flames and its crew perished.

However, the photograph below right shows "315" at Bergen Airfield after the May War. "308" returned unscathed to Schiphol. The crew of "856" consisted of Lt Swagerman, Lt Anceaux, Sgt Douwes-Dekker, Sgt Riemsdijk and Pvt Wijnstra. The crew of "308" comprised Lt Sandberg and Sgt Breemer; that of "315" was Lt Schoute and Sgt Lindner.

Fuselages under construction in the Fokker factory, left, D.XXIs, right, covered T.V fuselages. Once the fuselages were complete all welds had to be sandpapered by hand.

Above: Another batch of D.XXI fuselages. In the background C.IIWs and a T.IVA.

Below: G.Is under construction.

"Black" Gerrit Reminisces

Flight shed foreman, Gerrit van der Meulen – or "Black" Gerrit, as many know him – related some of the circumstances at Fokker's before World War Two.

Seven cents per hour

In 1935 Gerrit (then 16 years old) started to work at Fokker's as an apprentice fitter for a wage of seven cents per hour. To give some impression of how little this was, it should be pointed out that a cup of coffee during worktime cost 5 cents, half a litre of milk was 6 cents, and a herring 10 cents. Gerrit started by drilling holes into bolts for split pins from morning 'til night. Whenever a series of fuselages had been welded, all the juniors had to sandpaper them: "the black filth was in the back of your brains." They worked weekly from 7.30 a.m. to 5 p.m. with 30min lunch break. On Saturdays they worked until 1 p.m.; then the whole factory was swept and cleaned. The vices were sandpapered until they shone. "The foreman was like a god. You crawled for him."

And yet, we had fun

"And yet, we had fun working. We each knew one another, and it seemed that people had more to spare for their fellow-men. We also got up to some tricks. The uncovered T.IV fuselages of welded steel tubing were, of course, marvellous climbing frames – until one of the German foremen (there were quite a few in those days) came at you cursing and blinding. In the wooden mock-up of project 180, an intercontinental aircraft, one could play fantastic games. They never found you there. There were cabins with wooden berths in the aircraft. Of course, you were scared that you may be fired. For the bachelors this meant no dole, and you had to hold out your hand at home.

"Unpaid in the reserve"

Once I was fired, and I registered immediately at the labour exchange – without result, of course. When I had found work myself (for one cent more, mind you), I went to report this. The man in the labour exchange said: "Give me that card. Fine, I'll send someone else there". I had to wait (without dole) until Fokker received another order and needed me once more. Aircraft like the G.I and the D.XXI were made behind a barrier in the corner of the factory. You were only allowed in there if your name appeared on the list which was held by the guardsman (usually a boy). But when a new type like that first came to perform over the factory, then everyone was allowed outside to watch. That was sensational.

Fokker did it himself

I can remember that Fokker once came

Effective countermeasures to fight unemployment now and in the future

We are grateful that we, in our wage-intensive company, can offer a worthwhile existence to more than

1,250 labourers and
office employees.

As a flourishing company, of which the Directorate and technical management is in Dutch hands, our factory has continuously contributed to our national prosperity for 19 years.

With its 130 technicians, including 28 Masters of Science, the factory forms a centre of scientific and practical aviation technology. Its fame has been carried far beyond our borders and is still spreading.

Based on knowledge and experience gained over 19 years, we expect – in view of the unlimited prospects of aviation – that an increasing number of countrymen can be guarded against unemployment in future.

The increase of the manufacture of military and commercial aircraft of Dutch design is, therefore, of national importance, both now and in the future.

Text of a Fokker advertisement of 1938.

to the factory whilst they were working
n a mock-up for the gondola to go under
e G.I. It had been made from electrical
onduit with clamps and cardboard.
Which idiot designed that?" he growled.
le took off his jacket, rolled up his sleeves,
nd in no time had welded a neat gondola.

At last the Fokker factories had regular work. The number of personnel employed rose to more than 1,500 for the first time, whilst some 500 were indirectly employed in the supplying factories. The so-called "concertina" effect disappeared from the personnel strength. It was very common during bad times for a large number of personnel to be discharged when a batch of aircraft had been delivered. Whenever there was work again, they applied anew. During the holidays a number of persons were discharged and afterwards restored to the payroll. This not only lost them their salary during the holidays, but they also received no share of profits or gratuities. Some were discharged five times and re-employed within the span of a few years. This did not mean that Fokker was a bad employer. That was how things were done in those days. Fokker, in fact, was one of the best-paying companies in the metal industry.

To return to 1938; licensing contracts with Finland, Denmark and Spain had been affirmed as early as 1936. The factory area was extended, as was the hangar space at Schiphol.

Indicative of the international tension was the fact that an Air Defence Guard was organised at Fokker.

At the Paris Air Show a full-sized mock-up of the D.XXIII, an unorthodox fighter with two engines in the fuselage and twin tail-booms, proved a great attraction. The construction of the T.VIIIW torpedo-bomber seaplane was advancing, and the Naval Air Service ordered 36 of the type. Many designs were produced for KLM, but none was built. Chief Designer Schatzki left to work for competitor Koolhoven, and was succeeded at Fokker's by Ing Beeling.

ake-off of the T.VIIIW prototype. The Naval Air Service ordered 36.

he flight sheds on Schiphol Airfield.

nterior view. The aircraft made in Amsterdam-North had to be taken by barge right through msterdam and along the Ringvaart, to be assembled at Schiphol where they were test flown.

Test pilot Leegstra climbs into his D.XXI cockpit on September 3rd, 1938, prior to setting a new Dutch altitude record of 11,353m.

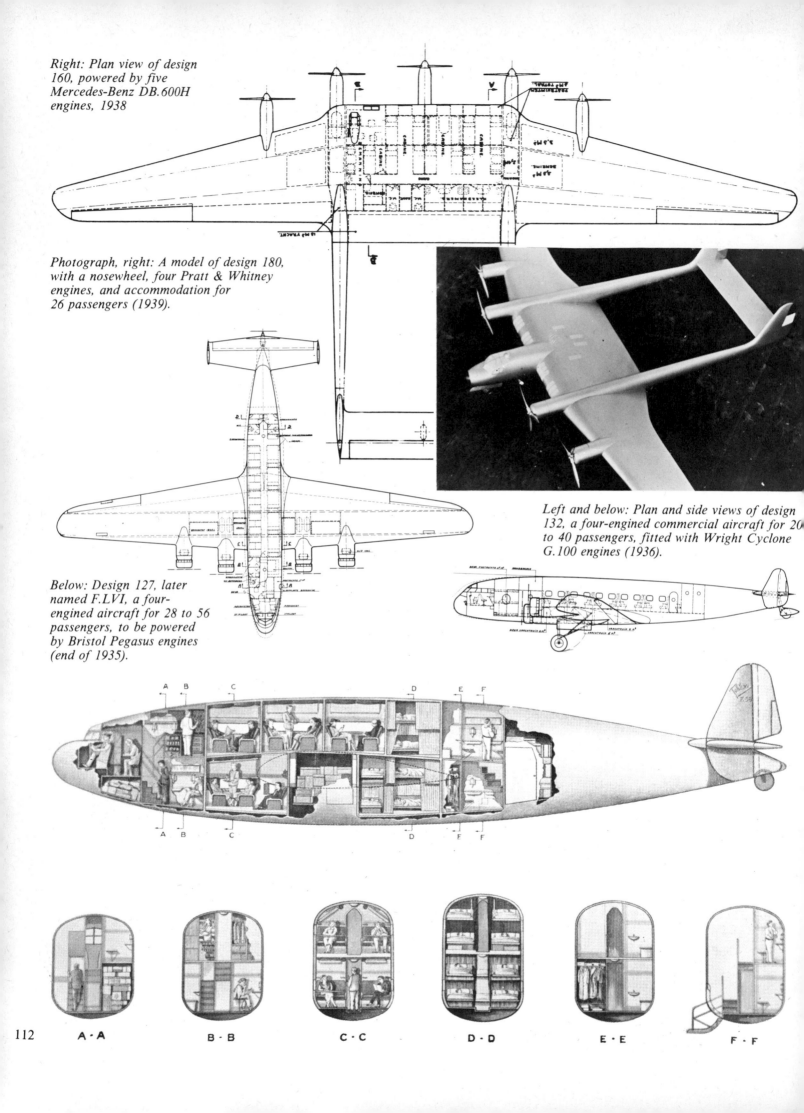

Right: Plan view of design 160, powered by five Mercedes-Benz DB.600H engines, 1938

Photograph, right: A model of design 180, with a nosewheel, four Pratt & Whitney engines, and accommodation for 26 passengers (1939).

Left and below: Plan and side views of design 132, a four-engined commercial aircraft for 20 to 40 passengers, fitted with Wright Cyclone G.100 engines (1936).

Below: Design 127, later named F.LVI, a four-engined aircraft for 28 to 56 passengers, to be powered by Bristol Pegasus engines (end of 1935).

A·A   B·B   C·C   D·D   E·E   F·F

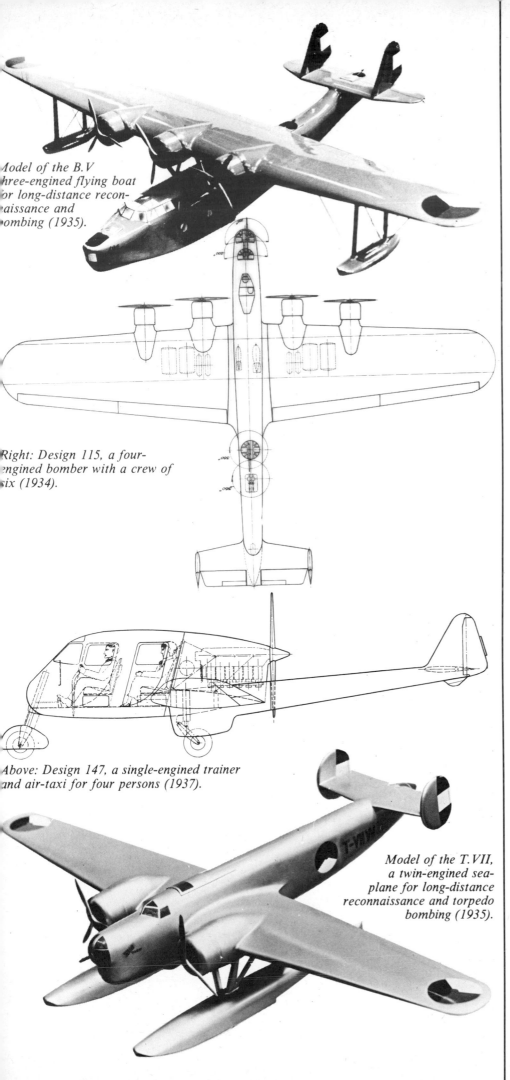

Model of the B.V three-engined flying boat for long-distance reconnaissance and bombing (1935).

Right: Design 115, a four-engined bomber with a crew of six (1934).

Above: Design 147, a single-engined trainer and air-taxi for four persons (1937).

Model of the T.VII, a twin-engined sea-plane for long-distance reconnaissance and torpedo bombing (1935).

Projects-Designs

A number of projects designed at Fokker were not built for various reasons. It would be going too far to quote all projects and the reasons why they were not built, but some of the projects from the period of 1934 to 1941 are described below.

1934: Design 115. Long-distance, four-engined bomber. The wing was based on that used for the F.XXXVI.

1935: Type T.VIIW. Twin-engined reconnaissance and torpedo-aircraft. The design was submitted by Fokker himself in 1935 to replace the T.IV. At the end of 1936 negotiations with the Naval Air Service were concluded without a contract being agreed.

1935: Type B.V. Long-distance flying boat for reconnaissance, torpedo dropping and bombing. At the beginning of 1935 the Dornier Wal flying boats of the Naval Air Service were due for replacement, and Fokker was requested to submit a design. This resulted in the three-engined B.V flying boat.

1935: Design 127 – later called F.LVI. KLM required a suitable four-engined metal commercial aircraft for the East Indies route. The delivery period was very short, and the problems resulting from this (plus problems of another nature) resulted in the decision to submit a new design (No. 132).

1936: Design 132. Four-engined commercial aircraft for 20 to 40 passengers. It was the counterpart of the DC-4.

1937: Design 147. Single-engine trainer and taxi aircraft with nosewheel and pusher propeller. KLM asked Fokker to design this aircraft in 1937, in anticipation of the introduction of four-engined airliners fitted with nosewheels. This would have enabled pilots to familiarise themselves with the ground handling of this configuration.

1938: Design 160. Five-engined transatlantic aircraft for 26 passengers, executed as a flying wing with twin tail-booms. It was pressurised and had a nose-wheel undercarriage.

1939: Design 180. Four-engined intercontinental commercial aircraft with pressurised cabin for 26 passengers. In 1939, simultaneously with the F.XXIV, an order was placed by KLM for one type 180. The design was carried on well into the war (1944). A mock-up cabin was produced, and the result of the pressurisation tests was satisfactory. The last version of design 180 had a wing with exactly the same slender profile as the one for the post-war F.27.

Above and left: The Fokker T.IX was Fokker's first all-metal bomber and was designed to succeed the Martin bombers used by the Royal Dutch East Indies Army. In September 1939 the T.IX made its maiden flight. It had a maximum speed of 440 km/hr, an armament of three machine guns, and carried a 2,000kg bomb load. In May 1940 it fell into German hands, but they were only interested in its Bristol Hercules sleeve-valve engines. The possibility of constructing a commercial aircraft derived from the T.IX was considered and discussed with KLM.

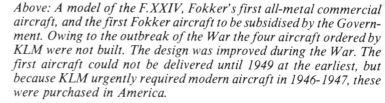

Above and below: Fokker's last fighter, the D.XXIII. With its two engines in tandem in the fuselage and twin-booms, it was very unorthodox. Powered by 520 h.p. Walter-Sagitta engines, the maximum speed was 520 km/hr. With Rolls-Royce or Daimler engines it would have been 615 km/hr. The D.XXIII had one big disadvantage. If the pilot had to leave the aircraft in flight, the rearmost propeller would have chopped him to pieces. For this reason Fokker was studying an ejector seat design.
Left: Ing Beeling, who was in charge of the project, right: Mr Gerben Sonderman, test pilot.

Above: A model of the F.XXIV, Fokker's first all-metal commercial aircraft, and the first Fokker aircraft to be subsidised by the Government. Owing to the outbreak of the War the four aircraft ordered by KLM were not built. The design was improved during the War. The first aircraft could not be delivered until 1949 at the earliest, but because KLM urgently required modern aircraft in 1946-1947, these were purchased in America.

Below: A T.VIII with wheeled undercarriage destined for Finland. The aircraft went, instead, to the Luftwaffe as a T.VIIIW/c.

ANTHONY FOKKER HAS DIED

**Holland's greatest Aircraft Constructor
passed away in New York.**

**BLOOD-TRANSFUSIONS WERE TO
NO AVAIL.**

(from our own correspondent)

New York, 23rd Dec.

Anthony Herman Gerard Fokker, the world-famous Dutch aircraft constructor and Director of the Netherlands Aircraft Company Fokker Ltd, has died after repeated blood-transfusions proved unsuccessful. He died this morning at half past eight (14 hours Amsterdam time), in the hospital where he was being nursed.

Some weeks ago Fokker had a nose operation, which, after an initially favourable result, became infected. A serious meningitis resulted with the result that Fokker, having lost consciousness several days ago, died in the country where he had lived almost continually during his last years.

We herewith fulfil the sad duty of informing you that Mr.

ANTHONY HERMAN GERARD FOKKER

Founder Member and Director of our Limited Company, after a short, but severe illness, has passed away in New York, aged 49 years.

Members of the Board and Management Netherlands Aircraft Factories Fokker.

Amsterdam, 23rd of December, 1939.

Below: On April 19th, 1941, the Management of the Fokker Factory offered Mrs Fokker-Diemont (Fokker's mother – who meant so much to him) a commemoration stone, which was placed on the family grave at the Cemetery at Westerveld. Seekatz (right) here offers the Commemoration Stone to Mrs Fokker (seated).

In the sphere of military orders Fokker had no cause to complain. But Fokker also wanted to recover his place in civil aviation. Between 1935 and 1939 a great number of projects were instigated for KLM, but none progressed beyond the design stage. On January 13th, 1939, it became known that KLM had placed an order with Douglas for DC-5 aircraft and that they were also interested in the DC-4E. To Fokker, this was the absolute limit. On February 11th he sent a memorandum to the Chairman of the Cabinet, Dr Colijn, to protest against the purchase of military and civil aircraft in America without giving the national industry the opportunity to produce competitive machines.

On February 27th an Advisory Council was formed and, following its advice, a so called Minor Contacting Commission, headed by Ing Ringers. On October 16th the KLM orders were announced in America, as well as an order placed with Fokker for four F.XXIVs and an intercontinental aircraft which was temporarily described as "Project 180". The Government was to subsidise the development with 800,000 guilders, and the construction with Dfl. 400,000 (see pages 112 and 113). The D.XXIII, which had proved such an attraction at the 1938 Paris Air Show, made its first flight in May, followed in September by Fokker's first all-metal bomber, the T.IX. The T.IXW also received its aerial baptism.

In Finland, where the so-called "Winter War" was being fought, the D.XXIs, C.Xs and C.Vs were fighting too.

Anthony Fokker died on December 23rd, 1939 in a New York hospital. He was 49 years old. His remains were sent by sea to Holland, where they were interred in the family vault at Driehuizen-Westerveld on February 3rd, 1940.

A few days after his death the contract for the F.XXIVs was signed – it would have been the first Fokker aircraft to be manufactured with a government subsidy, had the war not prevented it.

With the passing of Fokker a chapter of living aviation history had gone. Would he have been able to render his country a similar service in World War Two to those of 1914-1918 and the 'twenties? Who can tell? Five years later the world had changed completely. It is probable that the individualistic Anthony Fokker would not have been very happy in the new, purely scientific world of aviation.

Top, left and right: The Finnish state-owned aircraft factories fitted two D.XXIs with retractable undercarriages. This modification was much too expensive and radical in view of the advantages gained, and was not pursued.

Left: A Finnish D.XXI. Note the extra glazing behind the cockpit, which the Finns installed to improve the view. The swastikas on the fuselage and wings were light blue in a white circle. This Finnish identification is often confused with the German marking, which was black and diagonal, and placed only on the fin stabiliser, the Balkan Cross being applied to the fuselage and wings.

Above: A Finnish C.VE with strengthened undercarriage and a Bristol Pegasus engine. In the winter they flew with skis.

Above: This Fokker F.VIII was used by the Finns as a transport aircraft. It had previously served with KLM as H-NAEI.

Below: A Tupolev SB.2 bomber. The Finnish Fokker D.XXIs claimed many victims among these Russian attackers.

Below: The Finnish D.XXIs suffered losses too. This example is burning itself out after an accident.

Fokkers in Finland

Above: A Pegasus-engined Fokker C.X scout/bomber, of which some 35 were manufactured by the Finnish state-owned aircraft factory under license.

Right: Ing E.A. Järvineva, whose opinion of the D.XXI is reproduced in the right-hand column.

Below: This Fokker F.VIIA was donated to Finland by Denmark in 1941.

Bottom: A Fokker D.XXI, with an 825 h.p. Twin Wasp Junior engine. These were built only in Finland.

From 1919 to 1958 the Finnish Air Force had the following Fokker aircraft in service: three D.VIIs; one D.X; 19 C.Vs; 39 C.Xs; 100 D.XXIs; one F.VIIA and one F.VIII. From 1935 large quantities were purchased, and Valtion Lentokonetehdas (VL), the state-owned factory at Tampere, built 35 C.Xs and 93 D.XXIs under license from 1937 to 1944. Finland had also ordered the T.VIIIW, but the two ordered were taken over by the Germans in 1940. During the "Winter War" against Russia (30/11/39-13/3/40) the D.XXI was Finland's most important fighter. No fewer than 127 enemy aircraft were shot down by them, for the loss of 12 D.XXIs and eight C.Xs. Sweden supplied three C.Vs.

In 1940 two Norwegian C.Vs were interned and later put into service. The C.V, C.X and D.XXI also served in the ensuing war against Russia (25/6/41-4/9/44).

The C.Vs were gone, and they lost 22 C.Xs and 39 D.XXIs. The D.XXI had brought down 60 aircraft, but the type now served mainly as scouting and training aircraft.

In the Lapland War against Germany (1/10/44-25/4/45) another C.X was lost. After The Second World War the D.XXI served with the flying training school until 1948. The last C.X crashed on January 25th, 1958.

Ing E.A. Järvineva, has been employed by Valmet OY (previously VL) at Tampere since 1948. In 1941-42 he flew the D.XXI (with Wasp engine) with Squadron LLv 14 (VL built 55 D.XXIs with Pratt & Whitney Twin Wasp Junior engines, owing to a shortage of Bristol Mercury engines). He also used to fly the C.V. He wrote: "I was very fond of the D.XXI. With LLv 14 we mainly used it for low level reconnaissance and the strafing of enemy transports and ski patrols. We flew at minimum height to surprise the Russians and to evade the faster enemy fighters. The D.XXI was sturdy and could take an enormous number of hits without fatal results, due to its ease of construction. Our aircraft had the fuel and oil tanks wrapped in rubber and a 10mm thick armoured plate behind the seat. The four 7.7mm machine guns in the wing were ideally suited to our purpose."

Contributed by Mr F. Gerdessen.

Fokkers in Denmark

The I0, a trainer developed from the Fokker C.I in Denmark.

Hærens Flyvertropper, the Danish Army Air Service, used Fokker aircraft from 1922 to 1940. The first of these was a secondhand D.VII. They then bought two C.Is and two S.IIIs from Fokker, and three C.Is were built under license, the type proving very satisfactory. In 1926 the type I0 was developed from the C.I as a training aircraft, of which 15 were made. They then built seven type II0, a single-seater. In 1926 Fokker supplied five C.Vs, after which Flyvertroppernes Værkstæder built another 13. In 1934-1935 23 C.Vs of an improved type were built by FV, after Fokker had supplied a single C.V to serve as model. The first two C.Vs (R-1 and R-2) were used by the pilots Botved and Herschend in 1926 to make a flight to the Far East. Fokker supplied two D.XXIs in 1938, after which, in 1939-1940, ten more were built by FV. A start was then made to manufacture twelve G.IAs, but as a result of the German Occupation of Denmark in 1940 this production came to an end.

The Danish Navy has not used any Fokker aircraft. However, two F.XIIs were built by the Orlogsværft for DDL. At the time of the German attack on Denmark, April 9th, 1940, the four Flights of Hærens Flyvertropper had a total of 41 operational aircraft, including seven D.XXIs and 21 C.Vs. The aircraft were on Værløse Airfield, ready to depart for other bases, when a German attack was launched. One C.V was shot down and many other aircraft were destroyed, including one D.XXI and six C.Vs. The Danish forces were rendered inactive, and the aircraft were placed in storage, after being repaired if necessary. Antiquated aircraft such as the I0 and the II0, were scrapped.

In 1943 Denmark's occupation became much more severe, and the remaining aircraft were confiscated. The fate of the D.XXIs remains a mystery. They did *not* go to Finland. The C.Vs were put into active service with NSGr.11 on the Eastern Front in 1944.

Above: A Danish D.XXI with cannon armament.

A Danish D.XXI after a German attack.

Below: C.VEs of the Danish Army Air Service.

Fokkers in Norway

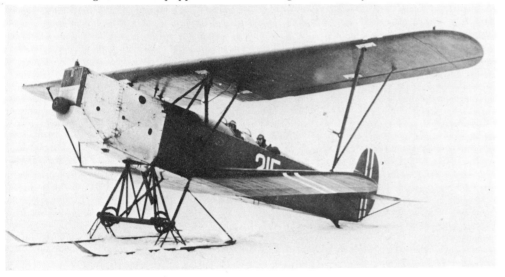

Above: A formation of Fokker C.Vs of the Norwegian Army Air Service. The C.V was their most important aircraft at the outbreak of World War Two.

Below: A Norwegian C.VD equipped with BMW engine and skis for trial.

In 1928 Norway purchased five C.Vs for Hærens Flyvevåben, the Army Air Service. During 1929-1939 another 42 C.Vs were built under license by Hærens Flyvemaskinfabrikk at Kjeller, and the type was the mainstay of the Hærens Flyvevåben. On April 9th, 1940, when Germany attacked Norway, at least 43 C.Vs were in the country, 30 of which were operational.

Due to the German air superiority over Southern Norway the Hærens Flyvevåben was unable to do anything. They were restricted to transportation flights and such like. Part of the flying training school, including four C.Vs, escaped to Sweden. In the beginning of May 1940 the remaining 11 aircraft, of which five were C.Vs, left for the North, where an entirely different situation existed. Hålogaland Flyavdeling (six C.VDs and three Tiger Moths) had been in action against the German troops around Narvik from April 9th. On May 5th, they had only two C.Vs left, and the recruits from the South were, therefore, very welcome. During the subsequent operations, some of the aircraft became inoperative, as they could no longer function on skis because of the thaw. For want of something better, car wheels were fitted on to two C.Vs, and these aircraft were used until the capitulation of the forces in the north on June 9th, 1940.

The serviceable aircraft then left for England and Finland. The two C.Vs flew to Finland, where they were interned and, after a major maintenance check, used by the Finnish Air Force until 1944. The four C.Vs in Sweden operated as target-towing aircraft with the Svensk Flygtjänst. The last aircraft, number 349, was handed back to Norway in 1949 and now rests in a museum.

Below: A C.VE with the Bristol Jupiter engine. The C.VD came into action against the German forces near Narvik in April 1940. When it began to thaw, and the aircraft could no longer operate on skis, two were fitted with car wheels.

119

Above: A T.V bomber of the Bomber Aircraft Department (BomVA). Nine out of the 16 T.Vs on order from the BomVA were operational on May 10th, 1940 at Schiphol. Eight managed to take off from Schiphol during the bombing raid, and even succeeded in shooting down a number of German aircraft. One T.V was hit by a bomb just before take-off. Five carried out a number of death-defying missions, usually without aerial cover.

Above: The bomb-racks of a T.V. On May 10th, 1940, these racks were still under test. Only two T.Vs were equipped with them, rendering them fit for their medium-heavy bomber role.

Below: The antiquated D.XXI in 1940, which scored a number of aerial victories in spite of their age.

Below: A D.XXI engine cowling with white mice emblem.

Below: A camouflaged G.IA during an alert. The G.I was the most modern combat aircraft of the Aviation Department in 1940. With its armament of eight machine guns in the nose and one in the rear fuselage, it created considerable havoc among the attackers.

Below: The G.I and the D.XXI were the fighters with which Holland defended itself in the air.

Above: The observer (rear) and tailgunner (front) climb into their G.IA at Bergen Airfield. During the May 1940 war, the G.IA was generally operated by two men, the pilot and tailgunner.

Below: Series-produced G.IBs. Destined for Spain, they were requisitioned by the Aviation Dept. Only three could be armed with machine guns and used operationally. These so-called "little G.Is" were to be armed by two cannon and two machine guns, but the cannon were not available.

Below: An air-raid alert exercise at the Fokker Company. During the war of May 1940 the factory was not attacked and continued to function, though some employees had to dig fox-holes or even sit on the roofs with machine guns.

Fokker was still feverishly producing military orders. Since the outbreak of war on September 3rd, 1939 the Dutch Armed Forces had been mobilised. Van Tijen visited Germany, and understood that Holland would not be spared. together with Fokker's financial director, Janse, he put three million guilders in a London bank for safe-keeping. However, van Tijen did not consider it safe enough, and not even in the American bank where he next transferred it. A New York branch of a Canadian bank finally supplied the security which he required. This money was to play an important role in the resurrection of the factory.

On March 28th, a Dutch Fokker aircraft claimed the first victim. A British Whitley bomber strayed off course after a flight over Germany, was fired at by a G.I over Rotterdam, and forced to land. However, the Dutch did not have to defend their neutrality much longer, because on May 10th, from 01.36 a.m. onwards, large groups of German aircraft crossed their borders and disappeared in a westerly direction over the North Sea. Optimists, thinking that our airspace had been violated for a massive attack on England, had their hopes dashed. The aircraft returned to Holland from over the North Sea to bomb the airfields of Bergen, Schiphol, Valkenburg, Ypenburg, Gilze-Rijen and Waalhaven and the Alexander Barracks in The Hague. The airfields at De Vlijt, De Kooij, Hilversum, Soesterberg, Haamstede and Souburg were strafed by fighters.

During this surprise attack 56 of the 71 operationally alert Dutch fighter aircraft (most of them Fokker machines) succeeded in taking off. By May 10th 49 of the 71 had been permanently placed out of action by bombing, strafing or aerial combat. The rest carried on flying up to and including May 14th, and the Germans had unexpectedly high losses inflicted upon them. They lost 231 aircraft over the Netherlands (excluding those that were hit over Holland and crashed later in Germany, although these aircraft were often damaged to such an extent that they remained grounded for a long time. German transport aircraft losses in Holland had a significant influence upon the course of the war, and were probably one of the reasons that England was not invaded by airborne troops.

Above: A gas-mask exercise on Bergen Airfield. At the rear is a Fokker G.IA. Below: A C.X scout, of which 20 were ordered in 1936 for the Aviation Department. In the May 1940 war they carried out several bombing and scouting missions.

Above: The D.XXI of Lt pilot Van den Bosch after being strafed. The sailor on the left kept on firing his machine gun at the German attackers without taking cover.
Below: Even the old D.XVII saw action.

Below: C.Vs of the 1st Reconnaissance Group. These aircraft, then 15 years old, carried out quite a few bombing and scouting missions together with the C.Xs. The slow, poorly-armed aircraft flew at extremely low level to guard against discovery. They called this "House-Tree-Animal" tactics ("hedge-hopping"). The large orange triangles on the wing did not aid concealment.

A T.VIII-torpedo aircraft of the Naval Air Service on the Brasemer Lake, a Naval yard from which several reconnaissance flights were made. The NAS had ordered 36 of these aircraft, but only 11 had been delivered when the invasion of Holland started. The R.3 took Foreign Affairs Minister van Kleffens and his secretary to England. Eight T.VIIIs managed to escape to England, via France, where they were used by a Dutch Squadron of the RAF (see page 129).

Above: This C.XIW was based at the Veere (Zeeland) Naval Yard during the German invasion. It ultimately arrived in the Dutch East Indies via England. Below: A C.XIVW. This training aircraft shot down a Messerschmitt fighter in aerial combat.

Above: A C.VIIW at the Naval Air Service Yard De Mok. These aircraft were lost during the German attack.
Below: A full-size mock-up of the C.XVW. This all-metal scouting aircraft was not built owing to the outbreak of war.

Leegstra (left) and Meinecke in front of the G.I prototype before the war.

A G.IB in German markings seen across the tail-boom of a second machine.

With the G.I to England

"Fliegerhorst" Schiphol, May 5th, 1941. Ing Vos, Head of the Technical Department of the occupied Fokker Factory, held an animated conversation with German members of the Board of Directors, telling them about the wartime flights he made as an observer in a G.I of the same type as the two in the factory, waiting to fly to the Luftwaffe the next day. He had heard that test-pilot Hidde Leegstra was to make a last check-out flight with one of these aircraft, and asked if it would be possible for him to go along. The request was granted. Relief welled up inside him. Ever since his return from the POW camp to the Fokker Factory he had made plans to escape. Like Hidde Leegstra, the test pilot who checked out the repaired Junkers 52 transports for the Germans, he was treated with suspicion by the Fokker workers. They were much too friendly with the Germans. In the Autumn of 1940, when first flying the T.VIIIWs for the Luftwaffe, they had schemed an escape in one of these machines, but the severe winter of 1940-41, with its thick ice, had put an end to that. Now on May 5th, 1941, it was "now or never". There was a solid cloud-layer, and the next day, after the delivery of the G.Is, their chance would be lost for-ever. Just before the men climbed into the aircraft, a high-ranking officer of the "delivery commission" became suspicious. After a long talk, the flight was allowed, on the grounds of Leegstra's reliability. At 16.20hr the two men started the engines (tanks full, thanks to the "escape" committee, as the regulations allowed only sufficient fuel for a flight of half an hour's duration).

They took off shadowed by another armed G.I, flown by the German test pilot Emil Meinecke. As they had announced beforehand, they flew in the direction of the IJssel Lake, where they performed some aerobatics. Quite unexpectedly, they disappeared into the clouds. Meinecke lost them and reported that the G.I, probably during one of these irresponsible manoeuvres, had crashed into the IJssel Lake. The G.I had meanwhile set course for England, where it was attacked by three Hurricanes near the coast. Leegstra managed to evade them, and they were soon over the East Suffolk coast, where they were fired at from the ground. Leegstra had already decided to put the aeroplane down in the first convenient field when he saw one between the trees which was not under cover of fire. He lowered the undercarriage and landed. The two escapers alighted from the aircraft as fast as possible, and stood next to it with their hands raised, shouting: "Don't shoot. We are not Germans." Fortunately, the area was being guarded by the Regular Army rather than the trigger-happy Home Guards or by the Poles, in which case they would probably not have been given the opportunity to prove that they were Dutch. After a few days in captivity both men were released. Vos received pilot's training and became an instructor with the RAF. Leegstra, after spending some time as an RAF instructor, went to America, where he occupied an important post in the Netherlands Purchasing Commission, responsible for purchasing aircraft for the Government of the Dutch East Indies, among others. After the war he went to KLM as technical representative. The G.I was examined at Farnborough and was then handed over to Miles Aircraft to test the influence of climate on wooden aircraft structures.

The escape-aircraft of Leegstra and Vos in British markings.

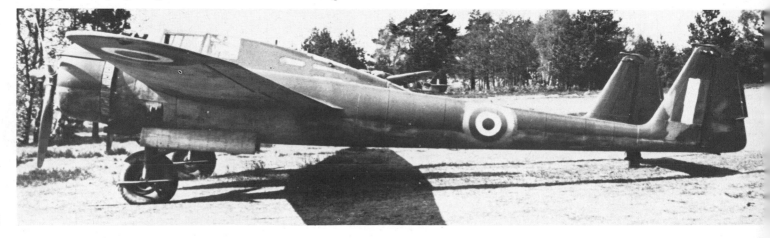

An S.11 Instructor post-war training aircraft for the Royal Netherlands Air Force (KLu)

THIJS POSTMA

FOKKER *S.13*

FOKKER S . *Mach-Trainer*

Wijbert Lindeman (with light overalls) standing next to a German "Factory Protector".

From left to right: standing, T.H. Leegstra, the Hon J.G. Beelaerts van Blokland, Bart., E.W. Boomsma. Seated, Wijbert Lindeman, Ing P.J. Vos, and Govert Steen.

Escape by T.VIIIW

One of the men in the Fokker Factory who helped Leegstra and Vos to escape was Wijbert Lindeman. Together with the resistance leader Lenglet he devised a plan to fly to England with at least ten members of the resistance. However, the pilot who was to fly the Junkers Ju 52 aircraft let them down at the very last minute, and someone in the group suggested Govert Steen as pilot.

Steen was working illegally as an apprentice for Fokker through the intervention of Mr Vos, and had been permitted to join the group by Lenglet. In the meantime it had become impossible to highjack a Ju 52. In April 1941 Lindeman discovered another possibility. In Minerva Harbour in Amsterdam was a new T.VIIIW, of which he knew all the "ins and outs". It was decided that Govert Steen would fly the aircraft, with Lindeman as adviser. Lots were drawn, and the Hon J.G. Beelaerts

van Blokland, Bart. and Wim Boomsma were the lucky ones. The flight was to take place on April 14th, 1941, but had to be postponed. After the successful escape of Leegstra and Vos in a G.I on May 5th, 1941, postponement was no longer possible for Steen and Lindeman. That same evening they went to Minerva Harbour and waited for darkness, hidden under a bridge. They then inflated a small canvas raft which Beelaerts had brought in a small suitcase, and rowed to the T.VIIIW. Whilst they were readying the aircraft for flight, a German patrol-boat passed by. The men pressed themselves against the floor of the cabin and the boat eventually pulled away. At the crack of dawn the engines were started, but one stalled. With one float still attached to a mooring cable, the T.VIIW started to taxi in circles. Boomsma threw off the cable and climbed aboard whilst the second engine was restarted. The numer-

ous German guards on the shore still took no notice. Steen cruised slowly through the harbour to get the engines to the correct temperature. After a hair-raising take-off, when he missed the Hem-bridge by an inch, the seaplane was airborne. It was Steen's first time at the controls of a seaplane. South of Zandvoort they were shot at by ack-ack guns, but it was obvious that they had been alerted too late and did not have time to aim properly. After more than an hour they reached the English coast between Folkestone and Dover, where the English now proceeded to shoot at them. Steen landed at once, and the four men, waving a Dutch flag, climbed out of the cabin. The date was May 6th, 1941. Steen died on June 5th, 1942 as an RAF fighter pilot. Jan Hof wrote a book about this escape, entitled: *Don't Shoot, We're Dutch,* which was published by Omniboek, The Hague, in 1978.

A German T.VIII of the type that Steen, Lindeman, Boomsma and Beelaerts van Blokland used for their escape.

Brochure of the S.14 Mach-trainer of 1951. Drawing by H.A. Somberg.

Above: A G.IB captured by the Germans, but still in Dutch markings. Various G.Is were captured from the Aviation Department; four were in storage and five were almost completed at the Fokker works. These aircraft were completed, repaired or modified and handed over to the Luftwaffe for advance training. By passive resistance the Fok-ker employees delayed the work for as long as possible. As a safety *precaution the aircraft were to be test flown by Dutch pilots under German supervision.*

Below: The T.VIIIWs which were under construction for Finland were also completed and used by the Luftwaffe in the Mediterranean area.

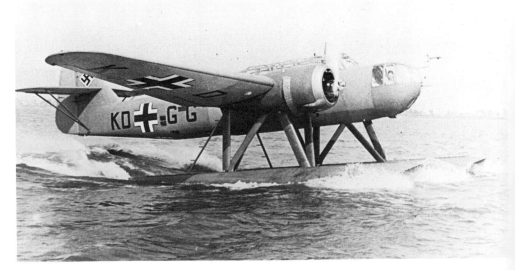

Above: A C.VE of the "Nachtslachtgruppe" 11. NSGr.11 was an Estonian section of the Luftwaffe, operating on the Eastern Front. Using ancient aircraft, they carried out bombing raids on the Russian lines. In March 1944 3/NSGr.11 received approximately 20 C.VEs of Danish origin. The pilots, some of whom came from Estonia, were very satisfied with the C.V. They suffered no losses in action, but minor accidents and cannibalisation had reduced their number to 7 by September 1944. NSGr.11 was then withdrawn from Estonia, which was the reason that ten men escaped to Sweden in three aircraft (two of which were C.Vs) in October 1944.

Right: A T.VIIIW like that used for the escape of Steen et al.

Fokker Aircraft in the RAF

Above: The F.XXII G-AFZP with the RAF. It was the former PH-AJP Papegaai of KLM. It was used as a navigation trainer, together with yet another former KLM F.XXII and the sole KLM F.XXXVI.

Below: A patrol of T.VIIIWs of RAF Coastal Command.

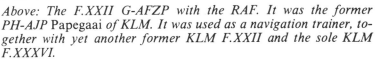

Above: F.XXII G-AFZR of the RAF. This was the former PH-AJR Roerdomp of KLM.

Left: A T.VIIIW of 320 (Dutch) Squadron, RAF. Eight T.VIIIWs escaped to England, where they operated from Pembroke Dock. The last aircraft was decommissioned at the end of 1940. H. Schaper (later General) made a flight to occupied Holland in one of these T.VIIIWs to pick up four agents from the Tjeuker Lake. No contact was made, and they returned the following night. The mission was betrayed, and the T.VIIIW only just escaped amid a hail of machine gun fire and searchlights.

Fokker Aircraft in the Dutch East Indies

Above: Fokker T.IVAs in formation with Ryan training aircraft of the Naval Air Service in the Dutch East Indies. At the end of 1941 the NAS had ten T.IVAs. In March 1942 the remaining aircraft were destroyed by the NAS themselves. The T.IV in its basic form had made its maiden flight as far back as 1927.

Above: C.XIW on board HM Flotilla-leader Tromp.

Below: Another photograph of the East Indies T.IVAs together with the Ryans.

Above: C.X scout/bomber aircraft of the Royal Dutch East Indies Army. The C.X had been designed for this force in 1933, and the last aircraft was delivered in 1936. After a few years, having become outdated, they were put into service with the flying training school, where they performed very well.

The Occupied Fokker Factory

Above and below: After the fighting of May 1940, a large number of damaged Junkers 52s were lying around, and recovery crews formed of Fokker personnel were sent out to recover them for repair.

Below: Junkers 52s in the new T.VIIIW shed, where the T.IX was suspended from the ceiling. On the night of October 7/8, 1940 two fragmentation bombs fell on this shed, causing a great deal of damage.

Immediately upon occupation, the Fokker company was compelled to work for German aviation under the orders of the Reichsluftfahrtministerium (Governmental Ministry for Aviation). The management launched a protest against this action with the Governor for the Netherlands (Reichskommissar).

At the beginning of July the commissioner-delegate, Mr C.G. Vatier Kraane, and commissioner Dr De Vlugt were requested to visit the German authorities in Amsterdam. They were informed that Mr F.W. Seekatz, then Head of the Export Department, would be appointed Director over and above van Tijen. The latter was arrested by the Sicherheitsdienst (SS – Security Service) on November 29th, 1940, being accused of "Feindbegunstigung" (fraternisation with the enemy). In February 1941 he was released owing to lack of evidence, after which he requested dismissal of his own accord. Shortly afterwards, as described earlier, Vos and Leegstra escaped in a G.I to be followed a day later by Steen and Linderman in a T.VIIIW. Presumably as the result of van Tijen's arrest and the escapes, the German Dr E.W. Pleines was appointed as Technical Director.

From then onwards, more and more Germans were appointed to leading positions so that by the end of 1941 the factory was almost completely in German hands.
The Werkschutz (Security Guards) and the German plain clothes policemen received Pleines' particular attention. Verwalter (Superintendent) Seekatz, Fokker's assistant in better days, had helped many of the Dutch employees out of difficulties, but he could not prevent van Tijen being sent to Buchenwald concentration camp in March 1943.

The personnel was increased from 1,750 men in July 1940 to 5,450 in 1943, but productivity decreased drastically. Not only was "passive resistance" in action, but several of the employees were arrested for sabotage, espionage and similar activities. Seven employees were sentenced to death, one being pardoned and the others shot. The design office at first worked on the construction of the F.XXIVs for KLM but soon Junkers and Messerschmitt tried to

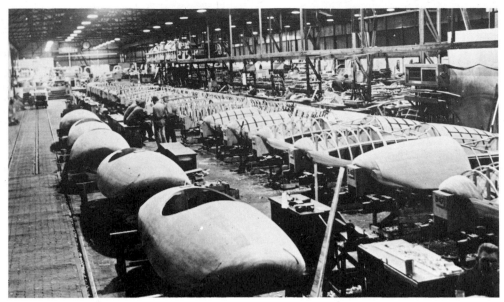

Above: Manufacture of "Schneekufen" (skis) for Junkers 88s. They were rejected, and many Fokker employees made fishing boats from them.

Above: A wooden stabiliser for the Bf 109. An order for 300 was to follow, but failed to materialise.

Above: Stress test on a wooden Bf 109 stabiliser, December 14th, 1942. This component was, however, not fitted to the Bf 109.

annexe Fokker's design office. Thanks to subversive support from Junkers, the technical staff managed to remain in Amsterdam.

On the morning of July 17th, 1943, Amsterdam-North was bombed by the Allies. The factory was not hit, but approximately 150 deaths were caused among the civilian population. Eight days later, on July 25th, another bombing raid followed, carried out by RAF Mitchells. This time a great deal of damage was done to the factory. On December 13th American bombers dropped 400 tons of bombs on targets in the vicinity of Amsterdam, once again hitting the Fokker works. After the raid of July 25th, decentralisation was commenced immediately for all departments of the factory. On a dispersal plan of November 1943 at least 48 different sites can be seen – in Amsterdam and its neighbourhood; in Edam, Weesp, Hilversum, Helmond, Purmerend, Muiden, Landsmeer, Oostzaan and Leiden.

In 1944 the Germans fixed firm prices for Fokker. At that time it was common to pay the cost price, and because of the labourers' sabotage this system proved very costly to the Germans.

In general, the Dutch management tried to eke out the factory equipment and stocks of raw materials as much as possible during the war, so that sufficient equipment would be available to recommence normal production at the war's end. In September 1944, however, the Fokker factory was stripped bare under the leadership of Dr Pleines. On "Mad Tuesday" (September 5th, 1944), all the German employees fled eastwards to Germany, except Seekatz. The management was temporarily taken over by Beeling, During and Hellebrekers. Seekatz refuse to co-operate with the stripping of the factory, thereby taking a grave personal risk. By the time the war ended the Fokker factory had been totally dismantled.

During the occupation the following items were delivered to the *Luftwaffe*:
26 T.VIIIWs and 26 G.I aircraft (completion only); 702 Bücker Bü 181B Bestmann training aircraft and 66 Arado Ar 196 seaplanes; 348 wings, 616 ailerons and 190 trim-tabs for DFS gliders; 377 sets of skis for Ju 88s (which were all rejected); 66 sets of floats and 200 sets of float undercarriages for Ju 52s, as well as a number of control surfaces; 60 "utility engines" and 64 oil-tanks for Ju 252s. In addition, 685 engine blocks and 60 unfinished engine mounts for the Ju 52 were welded, and 25 Do 24 flying boats went through their final production stage.

Left: Trials of the "utility engine" DB.600 near the Fokker factory. This powerplant was intended for the Ju 252.

Right: The final production stage of the Do24 flying boats. Components for these aircraft were made at Aviolanda and De Schelde.

Below: The Bücker Bü 181B Bestmann was built in large numbers by Fokker during the war. Of mixed construction (wood and steel tubing), some 702 were built, and they were test flown at Hilversum airfield. The photograph below that shows a Bestmann with wings removed for transport from Amsterdam to Hilversum by trailer.

Below: The Arado Ar 196 was also of composite structure. Fokker built 66 of these, comprising 42 Ar 196A.3s and 24 Ar 196A.5s. The components were made in France by SNCASO.

Fokker happened to be a very good escape address for people sent to Germany as forced labourers. By means of the factory's apprentice school at the Meeuwenlaan in Amsterdam-North, hundreds of evaders were given papers and work. Among them were less technical people such as furriers and bartenders. Not only was it preferable not to be sent to Germany; you could sabotage things a lot better in Holland.

Below: A complete village of straw was built on top of the Fokker factory for camouflage purposes. When it rained, the not-quite-waterproof paint dripped on to your clothes.

Below: On July 25th, 1943, Mitchells of the RAF bombed the Fokker factory and caused heavy damage, despite the camouflage.

133

The Fokker float during the arrival of St Nicolas in Amsterdam on December 1st, 1945. Apart from this kind of work the Fokker employees also made the toys for the St Nicolas festivities in the factory.

The text on the float reads "Holland, Air-Power with Dutch aircraft" The employees were so keen to reconstruct "their" factory, that they would have worked free of charge.

Right: Three confiscated Ju52s were refurbished and made into flying classrooms for the Government flying school.

In December 1945 Fokker received its first post war order, for a total of 72 gliders for the Royal Netherlands Aeronautical Society (KNVvL). This was a most important order because it provided work for welders and carpenters and also for the drawing office, as most of the drawings had to be re-drawn to comply with factory standards.

During the war Dutch aviation activities had, of course, come to a halt. After the capitulation of Germany there were, with the exception of personnel from England and Australia, neither pilots nor aircraft available to revive KLM and Dutch military aviation. Gliding was the ideal means of recruiting and selecting personnel.

Right: One of the six Goevier two-seat gliders under construction for KNVvL in April 1948.

Below: One of six Olympia gliders built by Fokker.

Below right: Some of the 36 production ESG's ready for delivery.

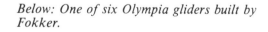

Above: On the Fokker float pulled by skin and bone horses in a flower parade in June 1945, one could read: "Holland Again a Nation of Aviation".
Below: The DC-3 Buizerd of KLM, a pre-war DC-3 which had escaped to England, is seen during overhaul at Fokker in 1945.

Below: The sad prospect offered by the Fokker factory after the war.

On May 5th, 1945, the war was over in Europe, and Holland no longer had an aircraft industry. The machines and tools had been stolen and the factory was destroyed. Thousands of people employed in aviation, including some 450 leading engineers and technicians, were unemployed and receiving retention pay.

The money safely stored away by van Tijen just before the outbreak of the war now proved useful. Van Tijen himself was found alive in Buchenwald concentration camp, and on June 14th he was appointed manager and controller of the factory. When possible, machines and tools were bought from England and America, and later from Czechoslovakia and Germany. Some stolen machines were recovered from Germany, where Pleines had used them to buy himself into the Mitteldeutsche Metallwerke at Erfurt.

Other machines and tools returned from very odd places. Employees of Fokker, for instance, had managed to sink a complete barge loaded with lathes, etc., into the river Amstel, and these reappeared from the deep. Gradually more people were recalled. Everyone joined in to rebuild the business, whatever the job. For example, a chief mechanic took pride in stripping the paint from a DC-3.

In September the Dutch Government made it known that, in principle, they wanted a Dutch aircraft industry combining Fokker, Aviolanda, and the aircraft manufacturing side of De Schelde.

The pre-war licensing and sales rights for the DC-3 in Europe were retained, and to meet the immediate requirements of KLM some military DC-3s were converted to passenger aircraft by Fokker. The Royal Netherlands Aeronautical Society (KNVvL) gave Fokker an order for 72 gliders, comprising 36 ESGs, 24 Grunau Babies, six Olympias and six Goeviers. A start was also made with the design of a primary trainer; the Fokker S.11.

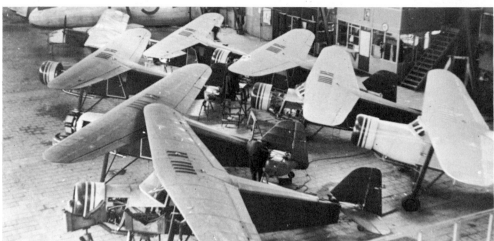

Above: This four-engined DC-4 was too big to be transported by barge through the canals of Amsterdam. Mobile shacks were constructed to protect the Fokker fitters against the cold whilst carrying out an overhaul.

Top left: Frits Diepen Aircraft Ltd placed an order for three S.IXs of pre-war design whilst awaiting the new S.11 trainer.

Left: Whilst awaiting the F.25, Diepen ordered eight Koolhoven FK.43 air-taxis from Fokker.

Left: A demonstration by Fokker employees during the commemoration of the strike of February 1941, when they downed tools. A special sabotage team was formed which set fire to the carpentry and paint shops, among others. Six of the team were shot.

Below left: Manufacturing omnibuses in the Papaverweg factory. Fokker made 75 buses for the Dutch Railways, and 248 Scania Vabis and 40 Saurer buses for Verheul and Company.

The drawings on the right depict the Fokker F.26 Phantom, an ambitious design for a twin-jet aircraft to carry 17 passengers and a three-man crew in a pressurised fuselage. It progressed no further than the design stage.

Below: Another project that was never built, the P.1 Partner, a two-seat private aircraft with a nose section that tipped forward to provide access.

Above: The F.25 Promotor business aircraft, of which 100 were ordered by Frits Diepen for his air-taxi company and sales purposes. The F.25 was exhibited at the first post-war Paris Air Show and, after modification to improve its performance, made a demonstration tour of Europe. The press praised the aircraft, but the sales were disappointing. Only 21 were built, and not all of these flew.

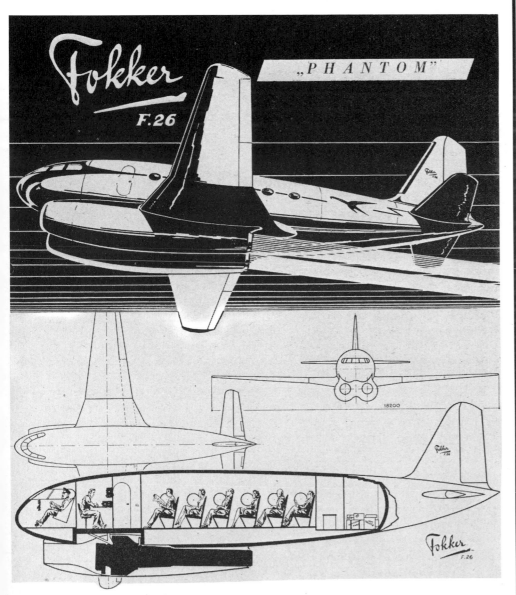

In 1945 the Dutch Government had stated that they considered it important that a Dutch national aircraft company be formed, but so far nothing had been done about it. In May 1946 the Fokker Factory had spent approximately Dfl.6,000,000, and it was obvious that this situation could not continue. It was due to van Tijen's energy and perseverance that, on May 14th, the Dutch government decided to keep the aircraft industry alive, but with the condition that a merger of the existing Dutch aircraft companies was brought about. The government was to contribute Dfl.2,000,000 for the manufacture of new types. Thanks to van Tijen, the workers in the aircraft industry were assured a more secure future, as the government promised that the pre-war fluctuations of personnel would never return. On September 1st van Tijen resigned as Director, although he stayed on as controller for the discussions on the forthcoming merger.

The daily management of the company was handed over to Beeling and During by the so-called "Controlling Institute".

On May 16th the Frits Diepen Vliegtuigen Co Ltd placed an order for 100 F.25s. This four-seat business aircraft was designed to the order of Diepen, who acquired the worldwide selling rights. At the same time Diepen ordered three S.IX training aircraft and eight Koolhoven FK.43 air-taxis. Although these were pre-war designs they had the advantage that they could be manufactured from existing drawings, and would bridge the gap until the arrival of the S.11 and F.25. The first foreign order Fokker received after the war was for the conversion of five DC-3s for the Finnish company, Aero OY. Many more followed, as well as conversion and overhaul orders for DC-4s.

Another order of quite a different nature was for 75 omnibuses. Some new sheds were also built.

On October 20th, the prototype F.25 Promotor made its maiden flight. A month later the aircraft was exhibited at the Paris Air Show, where models of a two-seat version, the P.1 Partner, and a 17-passenger jet aircraft, the F.26 Phantom, also were shown. Another model displayed was of the S.11, and it was announced that Frits Diepen Aircraft had ordered 100 of the type.

Above: The first prototype S.11. Note the different cockpit compared with production S.11s depicted in other photographs.

Above: A formation of S.11s of the Israeli Air Force, who bought 41.

Below: Italian S.11s made by Macchi.

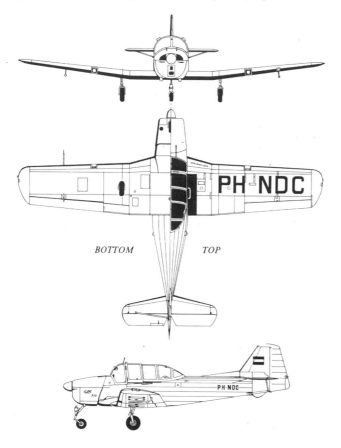

BOTTOM   TOP

Above: A three-view drawing of the S.12, an S.11 with nosewheel undercarriage. This version was not built in Holland.

Below: S.11s under construction in the Brazilian Fokker Factory in Rio de Janeiro. The S.11 was designated T.21 in the Brazilian Air Force.

A series of T.22s, ready for delivery to the Brazilian Air Force. T.22 was the military designation of the Brazilian-built S.12.

On February 1st, 1947 an agreement was signed between Fokker, Aviolanda and De Schelde's aviation department by which the long-awaited merger was achieved. The name of the new conglomerate was "United Netherlands Aircraft Factories Fokker", and its management was in the hands of Ing Vos, P.A. van der Velde, Ing Beeling and Ing van der Laan.

Fokker acquired the licensing rights to build Harvard components from North American – who, a long time ago, had taken over the American Fokker Factories. This led to an order from the Swiss Air Force for the overhaul of 50 of these trainers. Additionally, some Anson, Harvard, Oxford and Spitfire aircraft were overhauled for the Dutch Air Force (LSK).

By 1947 Fokker had become the biggest DC-3 repair company in Europe, about Dfl.9,000,000 worth of orders being received. The S.11 made its maiden flight on December 18th, that year, the F.25 received its Certificate of Airworthiness, and development of the S.12 and S.13 was started. In the meantime the "annual report" for the years 1940 to 1947 had been prepared, and showed a profit of Dfl.500,000!

At the beginning of 1948 Fokker received an order for the (licensed) manufacture of 25 Hawker Sea Fury carrier-based fighters for the Naval Air Service. The company was also contracted to build 100 Gloster Meteor Mk.IV jet fighters for the Dutch and Belgian Air Forces, but this contract was altered so frequently that production was not started until 1950, when a later version, the Mk.8 began to roll off the production lines. On November 15th the construction of a new factory was started at Schiphol. The personnel strength had increased to 2,000, and the new building was designed to accommodate 3,000 workers, with sufficient potential growth to house 6,000.

On April 1st, 1949 it became apparent that the merger between Fokker, Aviolanda and De Schelde had failed, and the controlling body appointed Messrs. Vos, Beeling, and During directors of the Fokker factory. On July 21st, its 30th anniversary, the factory received the prefix "Royal". At the time there was talk of cancelling the prototypes, but this danger was by-passed and Fokker remained a self-supporting company with a government subsidy, the expenditure of which came under governmental supervision.

One of the aircraft in great demand immediately following the war was a training aircraft for military and civil use. In 1946 the government ordered the manufacture of two prototype S.11 aircraft, and on December 18th, 1947, the first machine took to the air. Frits Diepen ordered 100, of which 41 went to the Israeli Air Force and 39 to the LSK (Luchtstrijdkrachten – Dutch Air Force). Fokker sold the Italian Macchi Factory the rights to build the S.11 under license, and, together with IMAM, they built 180 of them. Fokker also founded a factory in Brazil, where 100 were constructed for the Brazilian Air Force. A version of the S.11 with nosewheel under-

Above: As early as 1948 Fokker obtained an order for the production of 100 Gloster Meteor Mk.IVs. The contract was changed so often that production could not be started until 1950, by which time another version had appeared, the Mk.8. Fokker had built 330 Meteors when production ceased in 1953.

carriage, designated S.12, was not produced in Holland, but the Brazilian Fokker factory delivered 50 to the Brazilian Air Force. Later the factory was taken over by the Brazilian government.

Below: 25 Hawker Sea Fury aircraft under construction for the Naval Air Service. The last one was delivered on February 8th, 1952.

One of the best pilots Holland ever had was Gerben Sonderman. After his military training at Soesterberg he was appointed 2nd Lt. in the Reserve with the Aviation Department, and on January 23rd, 1939, he joined the Fokker company. During the war he participated in important underground activities, and from 1946 to 1947 he attended a test pilots' course in England. Apart from his job as test and demonstration pilot, he was also the personal pilot of Prince Bernhard, who became his close friend. Sonderman demonstrated various Fokker aircraft, including the S.11. The famous pilot H.J. van Overvest said of Sonderman: "... every time insiders watched him fly they asked; 'How in God's name, does he do it?', because feats beyond the capabilities of almost every other pilot were well within Sonderman's abilities." He died whilst demonstrating the S.14 on November 20th, 1955, aged 46.

Above: The S.13 crew trainer. This versatile aircraft could be used to train advanced pilots, navigators, bomb aimers, radio-telegraphers and observers. It was also suitable for the training of paratroopers and for aerial mapping. Test pilot Burgerhout made the first flight of the S.13 at Schiphol on March 13th, 1950. An intended order from KLM did not materialise owing to a gift of Beechcraft aeroplanes from America. The sole prototype was used during the flood disaster of February 1953 to photograph the inundated areas.

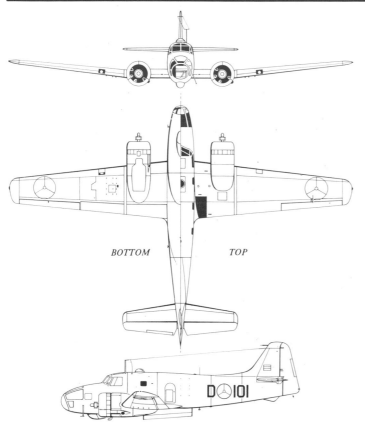

BOTTOM   TOP

Left: A three-view drawing of the S.13.

Below: The prototype S.14 jet trainer (foreground) in the new flight shed at Fokker Schiphol. Alongside is a Meteor Mk.8, and in the background, left to right, a Sea Fury, a production S.14, a Meteor Mk.7 and a Mk.IV.

140

The new Fokker Factory at Schiphol.

On March 13th, 1950, the S.13 made its first flight. There was international interest in this aircraft, but when, in May 1951, the so-called "Marshal Plan" became the "Mutual Security Plan" and the economic aid was changed to military aid, the Royal Netherlands Air Force (KLu) received a gift of used Beech aircraft from America. Fokker was unable to compete with their price, and the S.13 did not go into production.

On May 19th, 1951, the world's first real jet trainer, the Fokker S.14, made its maiden flight from Schiphol. The S.14 was a very promising aircraft, and the American Fairchild factory bought the rights for licensed production, but as a result of the MDAP military aid programme many countries were provided with the Lockheed T.33, a two-seat version of the F.80 jet fighter. The KLu ordered 20 S.14s the last of which was withdrawn from service in 1967. Fifty S.14s were to be built in Brazil, but production was cancelled.

In September 1951 the new factory at Schiphol came into use. In 1947 the employees had received a questionnaire in their wage-packet regarding the preferred location of a new factory, and Schiphol was chosen. The company's aircraft – previously produced in Amsterdam-North, taken to Schiphol by barge through all the canals and finally delivered to Ringvaart for final assembly and testflying – could now be built and test-flown at Schiphol, where the factory bordered the airfield.

Above: Licensed-construction of the SAAB Scandia in the Fokker Papaverweg factory.

Below: Hunter production under license at Schiphol.

In June 1952 Fokker received an order to manufacture, in co-operation with Aviolanda and De Schelde, six SAAB Scandia airliners. These were built in the Papaverweg factory, like the first of the Meteors. Later on the whole production line was transferred to Schiphol, where the Meteor was succeeded by the Hawker Hunter, of which 460 were produced, in association with Aviolanda, SABCA and Avions Fairey. When the last Meteor was delivered and the Hunter production began, every employee was given a packet of "Hunter" cigarettes. In 1952 the design and full-size fuselage mock-up of a DC-3 successor were begun. Market research in 1950 had started to determine the optimum layout for the Fokker F.27 Friendship.

1954

Above: The Scheldemusch, a single-seat sports aircraft with a six-metre wing span and an empty weight of 185kg. Its price was Dfl. 2,500, and its operating costs, including depreciation, maintenance etc., amounted to Dfl. 9 per hour. This small aircraft was designed in 1935 by the former Pander designer, Mr Slot, for the Royal Company De Schelde.

Above: A batch of SAAB Safir training aircraft under construction at the De Schelde factory in 1952. In 1954 this department was taken over by the Fokker company. De Schelde also produced the wings for the six Scandias.

Below: The DIFOGA 421 was built in secret during the war, but did not fly until the war was over. Its originator was Frits Diepen, Manager of Diepen's Ford Garage (hence DIFOGA). Frits Diepen (see photograph on page 145) became Commercial Director of Fokker in 1954.

On February 16th, 1954 Avio-Diepen became a subsidiary of Fokker, and on March 1st Frits Diepen became Commercial Director with Messrs. van Emden and During.

In 1941 he had secretly built a two-seat business aircraft in co-operation with a group of designers. After the war, in 1946, he founded the Frits Diepen Aircraft Co Ltd, which was to deal with the sale, repair and overhaul of aircraft, the transport of passengers by air-taxis, publicity flights and the running of Ypenburg Airfield. From 1948 to the end of 1949 the charter company Aero Holland was run by Diepen, together with the Steamship Company Nederland. On January 1st, 1949, the Frits Diepen Aircraft Co Ltd, became the holding company for Avio-Diepen Co Ltd, Aero-Holland Co Ltd, and Ypenburg Airfield Co Ltd.

From then onward repair and overhaul orders were handled by Avio-Diepen, which received numerous orders and numbered the Dutch, American, Danish and Norwegian Air Forces among their customers. In 1952 Ypenburg Airfield was taken over by the Dutch Ministry of Defence, and a runway of 2,400 metres in length was constructed. This enabled heavy aircraft and jets to fly in to Ypenburg, which was now situated on military land. An even older company in Dutch aviation, the aircraft construction department of the Royal Company De Schelde, joined the Fokker family on May 1st, 1954. De Schelde had taken over the aircraft construction department of the Pander furniture factory in The Hague at the end of 1934. De Schelde produced several designs of their own, including the Scheldemusch, a small single-seat biplane with a nosewheel undercarriage, and the Scheldemeeuw, the smallest flying boat in the world. Towards the end of the 'thirties they built a batch of Dornier Do.24 flying boats for the Naval Air Service, together with Aviolanda. Just like Fokker, De Schelde was ransacked during the war, and production was only re-commenced after a lot of difficulties had been overcome.

The company began by producing omnibuses, trailers and gliders. In the spring of 1952 the first SAAB Safir training aircraft, for which De Schelde had received a large licensed production order, left the factory. A batch of SAAB Scandia wings was also manufactured. At Schiphol Fokker built a large new flightshed with an area of 5,000 sq.m; the local personnel strength now totalled 4,000.

An F.27 "Maritime" of the Spanish Navy (Search And Rescue).

Above: The first F.27 Friendship prototype during its maiden flight on November 24th, 1955.

THE FRIENDSHIP IN THE AIR

Schiphol, 24 Nov. – The Fokker F.27 Friendship made a 34-minute flight today. At the controls was Fokker's chief test pilot, Mr H.V.B. Burgerhout. At approximately a quarter to three the Friendship took off, and exactly 34 minutes later it made a perfect landing at Schiphol. During the flight Mr Burgerhout circled a few times around Amsterdam. It was actually the second time that the Friendship had left the ground. Last Wednesday the aircraft became airborne during taxiing-trials, when it reached a considerable speed and flew at about 10 centimetres above the runway.

The trials of the Friendship, which was put back into hangar 9 at Schiphol, will be continued.

Co-director of the Technical Centre, Mr R.J. Schliekelmann, fulfilled an important role with Fokker during the development of the metal bonding methods. Encouraged by Mr van Meerten, he advanced this technique from experimental trials to the production status.

Below, left to right: Ing H.C. van Meerten, leader of the F.27 project, F.J.L. Diepen, commercial director, and H. During, financial director.

F.28.

The year 1955 is an extremely important landmark in the history of the Fokker factories, for it marks Fokker's return to the commercial aircraft market. On November 24th, the first F.27 prototype made its maiden flight. It was to become the most successful aircraft in the world in its class. While the DC-3 Dakota was a worthy successor to the Fokker F.VIIB/3m generation, the Friendship would prove a worthy successor to the Dakota. For its first trials the prototype F.27 was powered by Rolls-Royce Dart Mk. 507 engines, and in March 1956 these were replaced by Dart Mk. 511 engines. The first prototype did not have a pressurised cabin. Two of the prototypes never flew at all, as they were used to investigate fatigue, wing-loading and pressurisation problems (submerged in a water tank). Fokker's choice of a high-wing layout was surprising, because although all Fokker commercial aircraft before the Second World War were high-wing aircraft, the international trend was toward low-wing aircraft. Chief designer H.C. van Meerten, who was in charge of the project, decided upon a high-wing configuration because this offered more advantages from the operational economy point of view. The resulting low fuselage offered many advantages for loading and an unobstructed view for the passengers. Another significant feature of the F.27 was the widespread use of metal-bonded connections. Fokker led the world in the use of this system on a large scale. It was a courageous step forward, because everything new is initially viewed with suspicion because so little is known about it. Companies ordering the F.27 asked for special guarantees in their contracts. After Fokker had paved the way and proved that metal-bonded structures were not only aerodynamically cleaner but also much stronger and of greater durability, other aircraft manufacturers followed their example. Contrary to general practice, Fokker installed a pneumatic system for the retractable undercarriage, because air is cheap, fast and non-combustible. Moreover, the use of oil can lead to corrosion. All these decisions were to be justified, but in 1955 it took a lot of confidence to put such a project into the air.

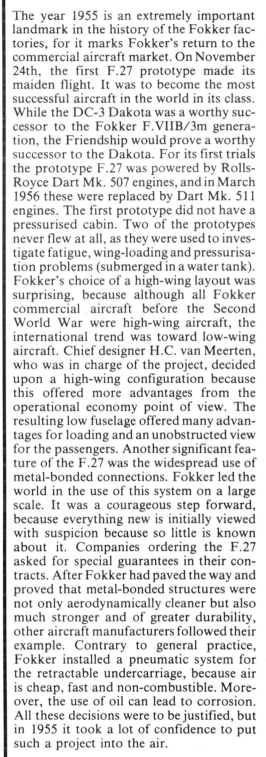

The Friendship made a prosperous start in 1956. By April orders had come in for 30 aircraft, and on April 26th it was announced that Fairchild would produce the F.27 in America under license. In March, an event occurred which was of great social importance. A workers' council was established in the company for the first time. Things had changed since the 'thirties.

The old factory at the Papaverweg in Amsterdam was finally closed in 1957. That same year a Dutch film about Fokker's life had its première, and proved an absolute flop.

On March 23rd, 1958, the first production F.27 EI-AKA for Aer Lingus, made its maiden flight, to be followed on April 12th by the first American-built F.27, for Piedmont Airlines. After the promising sales of 1956-57, sales in 1958 decreased so alarmingly that the future looked grim. Was Fokker to continue to produce aircraft that nobody wanted? Should production be stopped? To sell an aircraft that is no longer in production is a difficult proposition, but at Fokker they had confidence in the F.27. With financial aid from a consortium of banks and with governoent warrantees, Fokker scraped through a tricky 15-month period. Then a government order for 12 F.27s, including nine Troopships, changed the situation entirely. During the "dark days" of 1958-59 an intensive search for all kinds of work resulted in Schiphol building radar aerials, and Dordrecht producing "camp-trailers" (domestic buses). The factory in Rio de Janeiro was "adopted" by the Brazilian government. In 1960 the Breguet Atlantic was chosen as NATO's patrol aircraft, and the F-104 Starfighter was picked to succeed the Hawker Hunter, assuring work for Fokker in the immediate future.

Then F.27 sales increased. On March 21st, 1960, an agreement was reached with the Republic Aviation Corporation for Fokker to produce spares for the many F-84 Thunderstreak and RF-84F Thunderflash aircraft in service with the Dutch and Belgian Air Forces. Fokker and Republic also planned a vertical take-off fighter aircraft (which, however, was not to take-off at all).

Above: The first American-made F.27, built under license by Fairchild. The F.27 was the first twin-turboprop aircraft built in the USA, and an American F.27 became the first of the type to go into commercial use.

OWING TO LACK OF ORDERS

Fokker discharges personnel

(From our aviation-reporter)

Owing to a lack of orders for the F.27 Friendship – a phenomenon which, one hopes, is only temporary – the Fokker aircraft factory of Amsterdam is forced to reduce its personnel strength a little. Discussions are in progress with the workers' council and the trade unions. We learned from Fokker that dismissals will not be necessary for the time being. It is expected that the usual discharge rate, which averages seven to eight per cent, will be sufficient to solve the difficulties. This means some 250 to 300 men out of the total of 3,500 employed by Fokker at Schiphol. It is very possible that it will eventually become necessary for a number of personnel to be asked to seek employment elsewhere. Fokker has already entered into negotiations with other companies, e.g. DAF at Eindhoven, who need to replenish their personnel strength, and who would welcome the technical know-how and experience of ex-Fokker employees. At Fokker Dordrecht, the company at the Kilkade which employs about 800 men, the situation is slightly more favourable. Here, the management is convinced that the normal turn-over of personnel will be adequate. We have been assured that there will be no dismissals at Fokker-Dordrecht. Avio-Diepen, the works on the air base at Ypenburg, is not involved in Friendship production, so the personnel there will not be reduced.

Above: An advertisement of July 1957 for the film about Fokker's life. It was not a success.

Right: A newspaper cutting of March 12th, 1959. Fortunately matters soon improved.

Below: A radar-scanner built for Schiphol airport by Fokker.

Above: Roll-out of the first Fokker-assembled Starfighter, which flew for the first time on November 19th, 1961.

Below: Fokker as main contractor, built 350 F-104 Starfighters in co-operation with Hamburger Flugzeugbau, Weserflug, Focke Wulf and Aviolanda.

On January 1st, the 45hr week was introduced bringing an end to work on Saturday mornings. Factory equipment was also increased in 1961. On January 5th a 5,340-ton rubber press went into operation; the parking lot was enlarged by 238 parking spaces and Minister Visser opened the Electronic Test Centre on December 18th. At Dordrecht a new powerhouse was opened and new machines installed for F.104 production. The first Fokker-assembled F.104 Starfighter made its maiden flight on November 19th. Altogether, the so-called Northern Group, consisting of Fokker (the main contractor), Hamburger Flugzeugbau, Weserflug, Focke Wulf and Aviolanda, produced 350 Starfighters. Although these companies had never previously worked together in a programme of this size, production and co-operation developed very well. The first 30 Starfighters were assembled from components manufactured by Lockheed, and were followed on December 19th by the first aircraft wholly produced by the Northern Group. Fortunately, the Fokker factory was not entirely dependent upon the Starfighter programme. The sales of Fokker's main project, the F.27, were now growing steadily. On August 2nd, the 100th Friendship was sold, and all staff members received a huge cake. The French Breguet factory started to produce large F.27 fuselage components, and, in return, Fokker produced the central wing box and engine nacelles for the Atlantic anti-submarine aircraft, a truly European programme, which had as partners Fokker, Dornier, Fairey, SABCA, FN and Hispano, with Breguet as project leader. On August 31st, 1961 a ceremony took place to commemorate the 50th anniversary of Anthony Fokker's flights over his place of birth, Haarlem. Fokker's nephew, Mr T. Nijland, unveiled a plaque at the Santpoorter Square, and an exhibition entitled "From Spin to Sputnik" was organised in the market place. The festivities were reminiscent of an old-fashioned Queen's birthday: all the schoolchildren had the day off.

In 1962 the F.27 Mark 500 was introduced, a "stretched" version, with the fuselage lengthened by 1.5 metres and fitted with a large freight door.

The Trading Company Fokker-De Vries Lentsch was founded for the sale of reinforced fibreglass sailing boats. In 1963 the F.28 design for a commercial jet aircraft to carry 65 passengers was launched as a successor and sister-machine to the F.27.

For the twin jet Hamburger Flugzeugbau HFB.320 executive aircraft Fokker designers developed a most unusual wing configuration with forward-sweep (see photo opposite). In February 1963, Fokker entered into a contract with the American company Craig Systems Inc to build electronic shelters; a new flight shed was built; and the first components for the F.28 were produced. At Dordrecht a new assembly hall (0) was taken into use.

On February 18th, 1964, Fokker got the "green light" for the F.28, and Dfl.103,000,000 were made available by the Government. After a contest among Fokker employees the aircraft was named Fellowship.

In this period Fokker developed a house made of glass fibre. There was much interest in this development, but it did not go into production. A new autoclave was put into use in the metal bonding department. On August 25th, 1965, Fokker affirmed an agreement with the Indonesian government to establish a national aircraft factory in Indonesia, including the licensed production of 100 aircraft. Owing to the fall of the Government, this plan was abandoned. On November 17th the first order for an F.28 was placed by the German aviation company LTU.

Below: A newspaper cutting of October 23rd, 1963.

(From our correspondent)

SCHIPHOL, 23rd Oct. – The Fokker factories are seriously concerned about the developments regarding their new commercial jet aircraft, the F.28, which is now on the drawing board and should enter service with aircraft operators in 1967. A spokesman for the company stated yesterday, "If the government does not decide – at the end of next month at the latest – to advance the 120 million guilders which is needed for its development, production of the aircraft will be seriously delayed. We do not understand why The Hague is procrastinating. We only know that our competitors – the foreign aircraft factories who have a similar aircraft in the design stage – are laughing their heads off."

Above: An artist's impression of the Fokker-Republic D.24 Alliance design for a swing-wing vertical take-off fighter which was unveiled in 1962.

Dutch and American designers co-operated on this revolutionary design, which was to have a delta-shaped wing for high speeds. A surface which lay along the top of the leading edge in high speed flight could be swung forward to provide more lift at lower speeds. The aircraft's jet engine had four orifices the nozzles of which could be rotated downwards for vertical thrust and rearwards for forward flight. Unfortunately the project did not materialise.

Left: The Swiftsure sailing boat, of which the factories at Dordrecht and Ypenburg together produced 200.

Below: The Breguet Atlantic, NATO's anti-submarine aircraft. Fokker produced the central wing boxes and nacelles for this European programme. Partners with the Breguet factory were Dornier, Fairey, SABCA, FN, Hispano and Fokker. In 1978 it seemed that the Naval Air Service was going to order a later version of this aircraft, but the Lockheed Orion was chosen.

An aerial photograph of the SABCA factories at Gosselies. This factory and the one at Brussels became part of Fokker in 1966.

The unorthodox wing for the Hamburger Flugzeugbau HFB.320 was designed at Fokker.

Between November 18th, 1929 and November 9th, 1932, SABCA built 28 Fokker F.VII/3ms for Sabena under license.

Above: In 1962 the "stretched" F.27, the Mk.500 was introduced.

Below: Production of F.27 fuselages by Breguet at Biarritz.

On February 21st the decision was taken, in the furtherance of closer co-operation within the Benelux countries, to take over the SABCA works in Brussels and Gosselies. The Société Anonyme Belge de Constructions Aéronautique, abbreviated to SABCA, was an old acquaintance of Fokker. Since 1920 it had been the largest Belgian aircraft manufacturer, and the company had produced a great number of aircraft and engines under license, including 28 Fokker F.VIIB/3ms for Sabena. SABCA also produced several designs of its own. Like Fokker, SABCA had co-operated on the Starfighter and Atlantic programmes, and had also participated in the ELDO and ESRO space projects. SABCA was to retain its own identity within the Fokker organisation.

The sales of the F.27 kept increasing enormously. In May 1966 the number of aircraft sold (including those ordered in America) totalled more than 400.

New orders were also expected in the military sphere. On October 25th it was decided to replace the Republic F-84F Thunderstreak and the Lockheed T-33 T-Bird by the Northrop F.5. The main contractor was to be Canadair, but Fokker was to receive valuable compensation orders. The Service Department at Schiphol was extended by the addition of a "service centre" for aircraft maintenance, which, as well as the F.27, also dealt with other aircraft types.

On August 29th the Netherlands Aviation Company inaugurated the Netherlands air routes, using two F.27s hired from the RNAF. The history of internal air traffic is closely linked with Fokker. As early as 1920 KLM transported passengers between Amsterdam and Rotterdam. Up to 1937 the routes gradually increased, and immediately after World War Two when bridges, roads and railways were all badly damaged, an internal airline network was set up.

In 1949, when repairs to overland communications progressed sufficiently and it was no longer necessary to fly, KLM stopped the services. To run such a network economically, a very special kind of aircraft would be required. KLM found that the F.27 met these requirements.

In the meantime, a lot of work was put into the prototype F.28. In November a special F.28 committee (a so-called emergency council) was appointed, to ensure that the aeroplane would fly on May 15th, 1967.

1967

This year was marked by the amalgamation of Aviolanda with the Fokker company, which increased personnel strength by 1,200. After Fokker, Aviolanda is the oldest aircraft factory in Holland. The company was born on January 17th, 1927 and its first order was for the licensed production of 41 Dornier Wal flying boats for the Naval Air Service. Aviolanda is situated at the intersection of three rivers, the Noord, the Lower Merwede and the Dordtse Kil, and was therefore conveniently located for flying boat operations. During 1930-1938 Aviolanda produced eight Curtiss Hawk fighters. They also constructed welded steel-tube fuselages for Koolhoven E.K.51 and F.K.43 aircraft for the Royal Dutch East Indies Army, and repaired and overhauled machines for the Aviation Department.

In 1938 Aviolanda, together with the Royal Company De Schelde, began to build Dornier Do.24K flying boats for the Naval Air Service. During the war the manufacture of these aircraft was continued, but the company was not working its hardest! After the war Aviolanda had the same difficulties as Fokker, and lorry and omnibus coachwork became an important source of income. Conversion and overhaul of DC-3s and the repair of Harvard trainers comprised the first post-war aviation orders. This type of work increased steadily, and the former ties with the Naval Air Service were renewed.

Aviolanda had an important share of the licensed production of the Meteor, Hunter and Starfighter, and as part of Fokker, the company contributed considerably to F.5 production.

For the test flying of smaller aircraft, a short grass flying strip near the factory was used. Due to the ever-increasing size of the aircraft, a special repair department was set up on Woensdrecht airbase, where larger aircraft, such as the DC-8, were maintained or repaired. In 1950 Aviolanda invested in a 50 per cent share of the Dutch Helicopter Industry (NHI), which was later taken over completely. A number of Kolibri helicopters of original design were produced. In the years 1954-1959, the AT.21 radio-controlled "drone" or target-aircraft was designed and produced. The well-known telescopic passenger bridges, as seen at Schiphol and other major airports were (and still are) made by Aviolanda under the name "Aviobridge." Owing to the continued growth of this side of the business, a separate Aviobridge Co Ltd was established to cover these activities.

Above: Aviolanda at Papendrecht.   Below: Aviolanda at Woensdrecht.

Below: Licensed production of Dornier Do.24K flying boats for the Naval Air Service. The Do.24s did important work in the war against Japan.

Above: The first prototype of the F.28, PH-JHG, shortly before roll-out. The twin-engined F.28 was designed to accommodate 40 to 65 passengers, and the prototype was powered by a pair of Rolls-Royce RB.183-2 Spey Junior turbofan engines.

Below: Fokker's flight test team for the F.28, left to right, second pilot H.N. Themmen, flight engineer W. de Boer, test pilot A.P. Mol and flight engineer G.C. Dik.

Below: Roll-out of the first F.28 prototype on April 4th, 1967. It was a moment of great satisfaction to the many Fokker employees, who had done their utmost to get the aircraft ready in time.

The first pure-jet Fokker commercial aircraft was the F.28. On April 4th, 1967, the first prototype was rolled out after a period of exceptional effort by all engaged on the project. On May 9th the first flight was made, to be followed on August 3rd by the maiden flight of the second prototype. The first flight of the third prototype took place on October 20th. From the very beginning the F.28 was organised as a European project. The design and production were carried out in co-operation with Hamburger Flugzeugbau and the Vereinigte Flugtechnische Werke in Germany, and Short Brothers and Harland in Belfast, Northern Ireland, the agreement with these companies being entered into in the summer of 1964.

On January 4th, 1967, a contract was agreed with Fairchild-Hiller for the production of a shortened version of the F.28, the F.228, to be built in the USA. This aircraft has not, however, been put into production.

In the meantime the F.27 had become the best-selling turboprop airliner in the world. The Jordanian Company ALIA was the 100th customer for the F.27. Mr G.C. Klapwijk was appointed General Director, continuing a career which had included the post of secretary-treasurer of the Netherlands Institute for Aircraft Development and of the National Aviation Laboratory, followed by a period as financial director of Euro-control.

On January 1st the integration of labourers and office employees took place within the Fokker concern, and from then onwards one salary system was applied throughout the company.

Below: As chief designer, Dr J.H. Greidanus was responsible for the development of the F.28 Fellowship. Having completed his studies for his degree in physics and mathematics he had entered service with the National Aviation Laboratory in 1937. In 1951 he was appointed head of the Aerodynamics department of Fokker.

151

Above: Fokker F.28 tailplane assemblies under production at VFW-Fokker, Einswarden, Germany.
Below: F.28 wing production at Shorts; Belfast, Northern Ireland.

Above: A formation of three Fokker-VFW and VFW-Fokker products at the occasion of the Farnborough Show. From top to bottom: the VFW-614, no longer in production, the F.27 and the F.28 Mk.6000.

Top: The international Airbus, produced by a consortium comprising Aérospatiale (France), Deutsche Airbus (Germany) and CASA (Spain). Subcontractors at the time were Hawker-Siddeley (UK) and Fokker-VFW (Holland). At present British Aerospace (UK) is a risk-sharing partner, and Belairbus (Belgium) and Fokker-VFW (Holland) are subcontractors.

Below: The Lichtwerk Company of Hoogeveen became part of Fokker-VFW in 1969.

In March 1968, Fairchild dropped the F.228 project and ordered ten F.28s instead. Additionally, Boeing ordered ten aircraft stairs and The Naval Air Service ordered nine Breguet Atlantics, all of which provided work for Fokker. A new building of glass-fibre panels supplied by Fokker was put up for the marketing department, and the first pile for a new paint shop was driven into the ground. The first F.5 fuselage was handed over to Canadair on September 19th, 1968. In December it was decided to enter into a partnership with the French aircraft factory Marcel Dassault. Both companies were now involved with SABCA each having a 50 per cent share. The F.27 success story continued, with the sale of the 500th F.27 to Air Congo in 1968. On November 22nd, 1968 Fokker moved into astronautics for the first time, developing and producing spectrometer housing for the British Skylark rocket.

1969
On January 14th the official go-ahead was given for a preparatory study for a Dutch Astronomical Satellite (ANS). On February 24th, Fokker received the Certificate of Airworthiness for the F.28, followed on March 24th by the American FAA certificate. The first F.28 was delivered to LTU, (Germany) in February.

On May 12th Fokker announced that they were going to combine their activities with those of the German VFW company, and the holding company VFW-Fokker Ltd was formed, with the "Royal Netherlands Aircraft Factory Fokker Ltd" and "VFW" as co-owners, each with 50 per cent. This created one of the largest west-European conglomerates, with a personnel strength of 20,000. The same year the Dutch government decided to participate in the Airbus venture. As a result Fokker-VFW (as Fokker was named after the merger) was to produce the moving parts of the Airbus wings. The Lichtwerk company at Hoogeveen was also taken over in 1969.

1970-1974

Above: The F.28 Mk.2000 first flew on April 28th, 1971. This version has a stretched fuselage and can carry 79 passengers.

Below: The F.28 Mk.6000 has the same extended fuselage as the Mk.2000, but is equipped with leading-edge slats and improved engines.

Below: The prototype Short 330 (originally SD3-30) twin-engined turboprop for 30 passengers. Fokker produces the outer wing components and the wing struts. Short is a risk-sharing partner in the F.28 project, and produces the wings. This international exchange shares risk and spreads labour.

1970

In January, the spacecraft department received an order for the supply of sun-panels for the ESRO IV satellite, and Avio-Diepen received an order for 378 containers, having already received an order for 77 containers for Jumbo jets in

1969.

The industrial consortium Astronomical Netherlands Satellite (ANS) began design work for the first Dutch satellite in 1970. The consortium, which consists of Philips and Fokker-VFW, co-operates with the universities of Groningen and Utrecht, and with NASA in America.

1971

The sales of the F.27 in this year decreased to such an extent that the personnel strength had to be reduced by 1,750 (ten per cent). By the end of December about 50 F.28s had been sold; the break-even point being estimated at 200. A stretched version of the F.28 Mk.2000 made its first flight on April 28th.

1972

The sale of Avio-bridges was excellent, large quantities being produced by Fokker Drechtsteden (the new name for Fokker Dordrecht and Fokker Papendrecht).
The F.289, as the only aircraft in its class, came up against the latest, stringent noise-abatement regulations. By the end of the year Fokker had reduced its personnel by almost 20 per cent

1973

The year began with the delivery of the 100th Avio-bridge by Fokker-Drechtsteden. From May 1973 the Avio-bridges were to be license-built by the Fokker-VFW/Grumman Corporation in America. In the summer of 1973 it was decided to join in the development of the Shorts SD 3-30, a twin turboprop aircraft for 30 passengers.
Another development of the F.28 appeared in 1973; the Mk.6000 with greater span and improved engines. Its maiden flight took place on September 27th, 1974.

1974

This year Fokker developed important components for the Ariane satellite launch vehicle, and the Electronics Department received much work in connection with the project to improve the Hawk missile. The latter order resulted in a 50 per cent increase in this department's strength. Fokker also received an order to produce two air-lock compartments at a cost of Dfl.12,500,000.

154

1975-1978

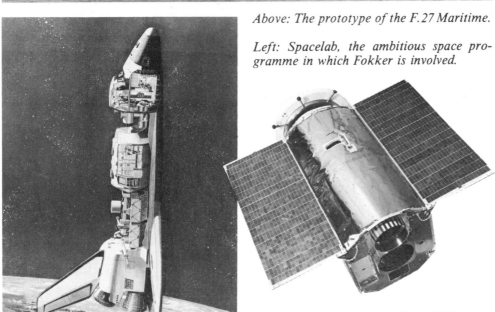

Above: The prototype of the F.27 Maritime.

Left: Spacelab, the ambitious space programme in which Fokker is involved.

Above: Holland's first satellite, ANS.

1975

In 1975 the F.28 Mk.4000, with seating for 85 passengers, made its first appearance. On June 7th, a joint statement by Belgium, Denmark, Holland and Norway stated that the General Dynamics F.16 had been chosen to succeed the Starfighter, and production lines were set up in Belgium and Holland. Fokker is to produce fuselage centre-sections and the moving wing parts for 589 aircraft, as well as completing the final assembly of 174 F.16s. It was announced in March 1975 that plans were in hand to develop a Super F.28 (or F.29).

1976

On March 25th a new F.27 variant, the Maritime, made its first flight. A medium-range patrol aircraft, it will complement costly and complicated aircraft such as the Orion and Atlantic.

More comfort and service is being offered to Schiphol-employed Fokker employees in the new company restaurant, which covers 3,000 sq. m. In December, the IRAS project for an infra-red satellite, for which Fokker was to make important components, was given the go-ahead.

1977

A labour-time reduction was requested for both Fokker-Drechtsteden and VFW-Fokker in Germany, owing to lack of work. The 1976 annual report showed a loss of five million Deutschemarks.

1978

The first F.16 component was handed over to General Dynamics, and on April 7th the production line started up.

A big disappointment came when the Dutch Government chose the Lockheed Orion as the successor to the Neptune, rather than the Atlantic M.4. This jeopardised both the labour of Fokker and its bargaining position regarding an approach to the French aerospace industry for possible risk-sharing participation in the Super F.28 or the F.29. On June 1st, Mr G.C. Klapwijk was succeeded by Mr F. Swarttouw as chairman of the board of directors. The Hoogeveen branch received orders for the supply of 940 shelters.

Left: An F.16 production line at Fokker's. 155

1979-1980...

Above: The Fokker factory at Schiphol alongside the Ringvaart canal by the Haarlemmermeer polder.

Fokker-VFW, the Royal Netherlands Aircraft Factory, now encompasses the complete Dutch aviation industry of six worksites, where some 7,300 persons are engaged upon various international projects. The Schiphol-East factory, housing approximately 4,500, is the headquarters of the management, marketing and administration departments, and also includes the production lines for the F.27, F.28 and F.16. Also at Schiphol are the design office with its technological centre, computerised milling machines, the metal-bonding department, the electronic department, the spacecraft department and the administrative computers. The moving parts for the wings of the Airbus and the F.16 are produced here. The two factories of Fokker-Drechtsteden provide work for almost 1,500 men and women. Apart from the production of parts for the F.27, F.28 and F.16, they carry out specialised work such as the manufacture of antennae and passenger bridges for airports.

At Avio-Fokker, which grew from Avio Diepen and Aviolanda Woensdrecht, some 1,400 people are employed on the sites of the Ypenburg and Woensdrecht airfields. Maintenance, overhaul and repair-work for civil and military aircraft form the largest proportion of the work done here, and at Woensdrecht they also produce the outer wings and wing struts for the Shorts 330. The ELMO division for the production of electronic systems, etc is also based here. At Ypenburg reinforced glass-fibre components are produced for the F.27, F.28, F-104, Airbus and Shorts 330, as well as radomes and fairings for Westland Lynx helicopters and window panels for KLM's DC-8 aircraft. At Hoogeveen, parts for space and aviation projects are made, as well as radar and telecommunications components. In addition they produce the LD-3 freight containers and shelters in series production.

Fokker's biggest success, the F.27 Friendship is still in production, and the new maritime version has already been delivered to Peru and Spain. Compared with the F.27, the F.28 is only at the beginning of its career. In June 1979, 145 F.28s had been sold, against 693 F.27s. In spite of these successes Fokker cannot afford to sit back and rest. There will come a time when the F.27 and F.28 no longer sell, and that is sufficient reason for the company to start project studies to ensure its future survival as an aircraft manufacturer.

Above: The IRAS (Infra-Red Astronomical Satellite), for which Fokker is the main contractor.

Right: Fokker is also carrying out wind-energy research.

Below: The first Fokker-built F.16 taking off for the first time on May 3rd, 1979.

Currently designated F.29, Fokker's F.28 successor is due to appear on the market around 1985. For the first complete specification for this new, advanced, commercial transport, Fokker carried out a market research with some 20 airlines around the world, including a few who traditionally operate Fokker aircraft. They will have played an important part in determining the F.29s ultimate performance and passenger accommodation

F.29 has standard seating for 115 passengers, but this can be increased to take 130 passengers. The aircraft will offer efficient and profit-making operations on short- and medium-range high frequency routes, and will be able to fly from airports with very stringent noise-requirements. It will be equipped with the latest type of high ratio by-pass turbine engines.

As of January 1979 the Dutch and German governments, the shareholders and the Supervising Board decided to terminate the then ten-year-old merger between Fokker and VFW. With this decision, which was taken in February 1980, the only transnational merger in the European aircraft industry came to an end.

Ing J. Cornelis, supervisor of the F.29 project, was born in Goes on September 24th, 1922. After studying aircraft construction at the Technical High School at Delft, with a two-year interruption caused by the war, he joined Fokker on November 1st, 1947. In 1952 he was attached to the F.27 project as project engineer. As temporary Head of the Design Department Mr Cornelis played an important role in the development of the F.27. A year later he was appointed Head of the Projects and Planning Department. From 1963 to 1972 he was Head of the Drawing Office, and in April 1972 he was appointed Head of the Design Office.

Below: The A-310 Airbus, in which Fokker will also participate.

... The Future

This book has recorded the history of the Fokker Company both extensively and colourfully. Whilst countless aircraft factories have been wound-up or have merged with other companies, Fokker, with its expertise and with much perseverance, has been able to survive.

At the time of writing the Company – together with five other aircraft manufacturers – belongs to the world's unique group of aircraft constructors. This position can only be maintained with extreme effort, but it may even grow stronger.

To this end continual innovation through a properly constructed and disciplined organisation will be required. For this process the involvement of every Fokker employee is necessary, as well as support from the government, political parties and the trade unions in Holland. Only under these conditions can a spear-head industry like Fokker continue to fulfil its social and commercial duties.

Within a very short period of time, decisions must be taken which could profoundly influence the survival of our industry up to the year 2000.

The first concerns the prospects and possibilities of the existing aircraft programmes; the F.27 Friendship and the F.28 Fellowship.

Despite the fact that the Friendship has already established itself, as described exhaustively in this book, there are indications that the production and sales of the world's most successful twin turbo-prop aircraft could pass beyond the magic total of 1,000 machines.

With regard to the F.28 Fellowship, the prognoses are a little more modest, owing to greater competition on the world market. However, it is expected that this passenger aircraft will remain an attractive proposition for a growing number of regional and local airlines.

In spite of the fact that future projects are continually influenced by a number of unpredictable factors, Fokker is already energetically scheming a number of new projects which will ensure the survival of the company when the present projects have been completed.

Plans have recently been announced concerning the studies for a successor to the F.28. This project, currently designated F.29, has been presented to some 20 airlines. Risk-sharing partners will have to be found, and, if all goes well, the aircraft will be available in 1985.

It remains to be seen whether or not the success of the Friendship can be equalled. However, based on the experiences gained while researching for the DC-3 replacement, fresh studies are under way for the modernisation of the F.27. The specific and stringent demands of this market, which were met in every respect by the F.27 – and are still being met by this aircraft – can only increase during the penultimate decade of this century.

Finding a suitable answer for all these requirements will be the biggest challenge to Fokker in the coming years.

The Sales Story

Much has been said about the people who designed and built Fokker aircraft so far in this book. The manufacture of aircraft can only be productive if they are sold and used, and – still more important – their continued production means the continuation of the Company; thereby ensuring the employment of their workers, provided that the customers keep on coming back for more.

Anthony Fokker became a skilled salesman from sheer necessity and he was also gifted with an extraordinary sense of publicity. In his time the specialised sales-process was far less important than it is today. During World War One, the demand for production was far greater than the demand on the salesmen selling the product. In fact, the aircraft sold themselves, providing they were good, and this aspect never worried Fokker during all these years of aircraft production.

KLMs director, Albert Plesman, could not buy better aircraft than those from Fokker after World War One, certainly not at such favourable terms. The excellent reputation acquired by KLM with its first Fokker aircraft continued the process but by the end of the war nearly all the world's aircraft industries were switching their production to civil airliners, and competition increased year by year.

Fokker's first outstanding salesman, Friedrich Wilhelm Seekatz, started to work for Fokker as Chief Engineer as early as 1914. His excellent contacts with nearly all the famous German pilots of those days, earned much goodwill for the Fokker company's products.

After World War One his talents as an aircraft salesman came to the fore, and Interavia later wrote about him 'as a salesman of Fokker Aircraft he acquired the reputation of being one of the best aircraft salesmen in the world'. Between 1935 and 1940 he was very successful in selling the DC-3 (Dakota) for which Fokker had the sales rights, in this way compensating for the lack of orders for aircraft of Fokker design. On pages 131 and 132 the sad story is told of how Seekatz was forced to leave the company.

Another Fokker employee who played a big role in the sales of Fokker aircraft was Ing B Stephan, who had been appointed co-director by Fokker in 1925. He became virtual Manager of the Dutch Fokker factory because Anthony Fokker himself was usually abroad in the USA. He, too, added considerably to the sales of Fokker aircraft between the two world wars and in those

Italian C.VEs. The C.V was one of the world's greatest military sales successes, and was produced in six countries under license.

Fokker with Seekatz in his FG.II glider at the 1922 Rhön Meeting. This was the world's first glider flight with a passenger.

Ing Stephan (centre with cane) with an Italian mission. Below: A three-engined F.VII, serving with the Polish airline LOT in the '20s.

The Fokker F.27, one of the great aviation export successes.

Fritz Diepen, the man behind the F.27s sales-success.

Daan Krook – the present generation. More than just sales-technique.

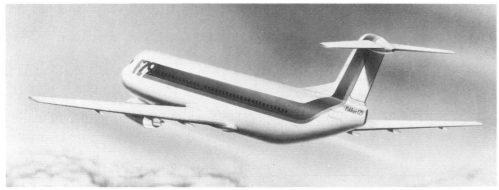

Above: The F.29, great things for the future. Below: F.28 in British airline service.

days it also became apparent that selling aircraft required more than skillful sales technique. Stephan was a schooled technician with a large dose of practical intelligence and was very cosmopolitan. This last quality was of great importance (and still is) because aviation was growing into a truly international affair. In 1935 Stephan left for Turkey to take up the appointment of advisor to the Turkish government.

In the last years before 1940, Fokker were mainly producing military aircraft. In view of the international situation the factory was only just able to meet the demand. After World War Two, only a ruin remained of the Fokker factory, but the sales organisation, international contacts and a service organisation were also in ruins.

One of the first customers after World War Two was Fritz Diepen. He ordered three S.9 trainer aircraft and eight Koolhoven taxis (produced by Fokker under license) for his air taxi and publicity company. He also financed a trade company and an aircraft repair works. For his trade company Fritz Diepen Aircraft at Ypenburg he ordered a series of Fokker F.25 Promoter aircraft and 100 S.11 trainers. This last bold order gave the Dutch aircraft industry its new foundation. On March 1st, 1955 Fritz Diepen joined the Fokker company and it can safely be said that he sold the F.27 Friendship. Alike both Stephan and Seekatz, Diepen was a thoroughbred, a cosmopolitan and an organiser and a man who had the sympathy of those he dealt with all over the world. In the USA, the sales were carried out by Fairchild. At the moment sales activities in the USA are carried out by Fokker themselves.

Fokker's total sales-organisation, including product support, at present numbers some 600 employees, under the leadership of Mr Daan Krook, a worthy successor to men like Seekatz, Stephan and Diepen. He joined Fokker in 1957 and extended the existing sales organisation considerably. After an interlude with Airbus, where he was Commercial Director for four years, achieving some noteworthy successes, Krook returned to Fokker in January 1979.

INDEX